Adventures *in* Nature

Speed and Comprehension Reader

A Beka Book® Pensacola, FL 32523-9100
a ministry of PENSACOLA CHRISTIAN COLLEGE

Speed and Comprehension Readers

Adventures in Other Lands
Adventures in Nature
Adventures in Greatness

Adventures in Nature:
Speed and Comprehension Reader
Third Edition

Staff Credits
Editors: Phyllis Rand, Heidi Mayfield
Designer: Mark Whitcher, Amy Tedder

A Beka Book, a Christian textbook ministry of Pensacola Christian College, is designed to meet the need for Christian textbooks and teaching aids. The purpose of this publishing ministry is to help Christian schools reach children and young people for the Lord and train them in the Christian way of life.

Acknowledgments

Special thanks is given to the *National Geographic School Bulletin* / National Geographic Image Collection for permission to use the following Old Explorer articles:
"Beaver Business," "The Blossoming Tulip Business," "Homing Pigeon Heroes," "Mollusk Mansions," "Nature's Sandpiles," "The Real Scoop about Ice Cream," "Summer Ice Storms," "The Valiant Horse," "The Windmill: Energy's Friend"

Also to the authors listed below / the National Geographic Image Collection for permission to use the following articles:
"Hippos at Home" by Charles H. Sloan, "Huskies in the Rockies" by Bruce Mace, "I Spy on Wild Animals from a Treetop Hotel" by George Crossette, "Lewis and Clark Open the Door to the West" by Charles H. Sloan, "Michigan's Magic Island" by Mrs. Patricia Robbins, "Pilgrims, Indians & Thanksgiving" by Joseph B. Goodwin, "Riding the Rapids" by Charles B. Cramer, "Red-Nosed Reindeer" by Mrs. Patricia Robbins, "Squid Tricks" by Mrs. Patricia Robbins, "Up and Away in a Hot-Air Balloon" by Richard M. Crum

"The Oyster Thief" taken from *The Oyster Thief* by Bob Devine, ©1979 Moody Bible Institute of Chicago. Moody Press. Used by permission.
"The Pincushion" from *Listen to the Animals* by William L. Coleman, ©1979 William L. Coleman. Published by Bethany House Publishers and used with permission.
"Storm Warnings" adapted from *Current Health 1,* March 1998, pp. 12 & 13. Special permission granted, and copyrighted ©1998 by Weekly Reader Corporation. All rights reserved.
"Trail-Makers," Parts 1 and 2, from *The Children's Hour: Favorite Animal Stories.* Copyright 1953 by Spencer Press, Inc. Reprinted with permission.
"The Trap-Door Spider" taken from *The Trap-Door Spider* by Bob Devine, ©1979 Moody Bible Institute of Chicago. Moody Press. Used by permission.
"Who Goes There?" taken from *The Soil Factory* by Bob Devine, ©1978 Moody Bible Institute of Chicago. Moody Press. Used by permission.

Photos: Corbis/Digital Stock: cover & p. i (brook in forest), viii, 3, 9, 26, 31, 37, 40, 55, 61, 81; Corel Corporation: cover & throughout book (sea stars, balloon, water drops), 7, 11, 13, 17, 19, 21, 34, 43, 46, 49, 52, 65, 69, 73, 91, 93; PhotoDisc: 15.

To Parents and Teachers

Adventures in Nature is a speed and comprehension reader. Although correlated with the *A Beka Book* Fifth Grade Reading Curriculum, the book is suitable for use in grades 5–7.

Beginning in fourth grade, the reading program provides specific opportunities for students to develop their comprehension skills. At this level, students have become personally responsible for much more history and science material and outside reading. Their vocabulary work is increased and they are expected to retain many more facts. Now is the time to begin stressing the importance of reading for information at the best possible speed. Because the reading program for the lower elementary grades stresses phonics and reading mastery, students are now ready to begin working on these other reading skills.

The best way to help students develop these skills is to allow time for much practice and to provide them with a variety of stimulating, well-written reading materials. The ability to comprehend is really the ability to *concentrate*. Teach your students good habits that will help them to concentrate.

It is not helpful to turn the development of comprehension skills into a "science" by spending the reading class finding core parts of the sentence, analyzing patterns of paragraph organization, recognizing related thought groups, etc. This is unnecessary if you have the right kind of language arts program. Spend the reading class reading!

Procedure for Using *Adventures in Nature*

The speed and comprehension exercises for grades 4–6 are purposely varied as to content, degree of difficulty, and length. They are challenging and interesting. Quizzes are included for each reading exercise.

1. Remove all quizzes and the Quiz Answer Key (pp. 157–158) from each book (or have students remove the quiz each week before beginning to read). Collate the quizzes, putting together the quizzes for each story. Quizzes will then be ready for distribution each week.

2. Make cards for the numbers 1–8 to show the amount of time that has passed. Each card should have one large number written on it.

3. Pass out *Adventures in Nature* and the appropriate quizzes. Have students place the quizzes face down on their desk. Announce the page number. Instruct students to find page announced, close their book (keeping their finger at the page), and hold the book above their head. When the class is ready, give the start signal.

4. As students are reading, time them with a watch or clock that is digital or has a second hand. Hold up a card with "1" on it after one minute has passed, "2" after two minutes have passed, etc. (or write the number quietly on the chalkboard). When students have finished reading, they should close their book, set it aside, and begin taking the quiz. No student should reopen his book after reading the quiz selection. For the first several weeks, allow time for students to read at the rate of approximately 100 words per minute. (For example, allow 8 minutes for a selection of 795 words.) As the year progresses, gradually shorten the time you allow them to read the selection. They should average *at least* 150 words per minute by the end of the year.

5. As they begin the quiz, they should check the number on the card you are holding and write that number at the bottom of the quiz. When all students have finished the quiz, have them exchange papers, and grade them in class. Each question has a 10 point value. Subtract the total from 100 to get the grade. Incorrect bonus answers are not counted. Have students divide the number of words read by the number of minutes it took them to read to figure words per minute. (You may need to talk through the process after first few quizzes.)

6. Have students call out grades and words per minute for you to record in grade book (Example: 90/200). Then have students pass in quizzes and *Adventures in Nature*. Follow this procedure for all Speed and Comprehension quizzes.

Pronunciation Key

Symbol • Example		Symbol • Example	
ā	āte	ô	côrd, taught, saw
â	dâre	ŏ	nŏt
ă	făt	oi	boil
ä	fäther	o͞o	bro͞od
ə	ago (ə·gō′)	o͝o	bo͝ok
ch	chin	ou	out
ē	ēven	sh	shark
ĕ	ĕgg	th	thin
*ê̆ (ər)	pondĕr	t̶h̶	t̶h̶ere
g	good	*tṳ (cho͞o)	virtṳe
ī	īce	ū	ūnit
ĭ	ĭt	û	ûrn
j	jog	ŭ	ŭp
ks	perplex (ks = x)	zh	azure (zh = z)
kw	quart (kw = qu)	'	little (lĭt′′l; shows that the vowel is not sounded)
ng	song		
ō	ōver		

*Note: For simplicity, the alternate symbols are used for ê̆r and tṳ.

v

Contents

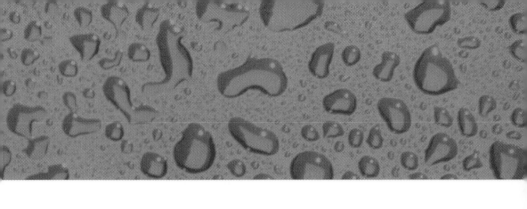

Life is so full of wonders that I've kind of spent my whole life just looking and staring. I've found that this is a great way to enjoy yourself. It seems that the more I observe, the more curious I become.

God, the Great Designer of the universe, has given us a world filled with more interesting things than we can ever see or read about in a lifetime—interesting things that are waiting for you around every corner and interesting persons that you may meet today. I hope that you enjoy reading about my observations and travels. Then go observe some wonders firsthand!

Pilgrims, Indians, and Thanksgiving

Joseph B. Goodwin

<u>Note these words:</u>
Plimoth: original spelling of Plymouth
Wampanoag (wäm′pə·nō′ăg)
Massasoit (măs′ə·soit′)

Three Indians and a palefaced boy helped make the Pilgrims' first Thanksgiving possible.

The first Indian, Samoset, walked into Plimoth Plantation in March, 1621. He found a weakened but brave band of settlers. Of the 99 who left the *Mayflower* in December, 1620, half had died on the bleak, stormy coast.

The Indian visitor must have stirred white men's hearts with his greeting.

Welcome, Englishmen!

Samoset had learned English from sailors who came ashore to dry cod caught on the Grand Banks. He spent the night at Plimoth, then returned to the Wampanoag Indian village with the news that unlike the fishermen, these foreigners planned to stay. An Indian named Squanto heard Samoset's story. Soon, he also paid a call on the Pilgrims.

Squanto spoke English well, for he had lived in London. Captured to be sold as a slave by sailors bound for Spain, Squanto escaped to another ship. He reached England where a London merchant befriended him, helping him return to New England. Home again near Plimoth, he found his entire clan dead from disease.

His own family gone, Squanto adopted the Pilgrims. The children loved him. He taught their parents the ways of the land, to plant corn, to fish and trap.

Squanto and Samoset brought the chief of the Wampanoags, Massasoit, to visit Plimoth's first governor, John Carver. It became clear that both leaders shared the same fear. Both groups were weak with illness. Alone, neither would be able to stand off an attack by enemy tribes. They decided to combine English gunpowder and Indian experience into a stout defense force.

The paleface, young Johnny Billington, paved the way for good relations with another tribe, the Nauset, who had attacked a *Mayflower* landing party.

Straying from home, Johnny fell into the Nausets' hands. They must have liked the lad, for they returned him draped with wampum belts, and the chief made peace.

With Indian aid, Plimoth Plantation prospered. When Massasoit and 90 of his men, women, and children paid a fall visit, William Bradford, the new governor, declared a holiday.

Working together, Pilgrims and Indians had survived dangerous times. That was reason enough to rejoice, and there was ample food in the storehouse for a feast of thanksgiving.

375 words

2

Hippos at Home
Charles H. Sloan

When a hippopotamus throws its weight around, peaceful streams turn into raging seas and small boats face disaster.

Adult hippos weigh four tons or more, second only to elephants among earth's largest land creatures. Unlike elephants, however, hippopotamuses prefer water to a life on land. Many unwary travelers have suffered surprise dunkings when hippos surfaced nearby, swamping their boats.

Unless startled into stampeding, hippopotamuses spend nearly all the daylight hours in rivers, lakes, and even ponds that seem far too small for the 12-foot length of full grown males.

The big mammal got its tongue-twisting name from the Greek words for "river horse." Its head vaguely resembles a horse's.

One explorer marveled that creatures with such a delicate sense of smell could stand the stench of hippo-packed pools hardly larger than puddles.

Most at home in water less than ten feet deep, hippos can stroll along on the bottom as easily as if on dry land. They may stay submerged for 10 to 12 minutes, then come up just long enough for a great gaping yawn and a deep breath.

Hippos also may spend hours closer to the surface. Eyes and nostrils conveniently mounted high on their heads let the animals see and breathe and still keep their bodies beneath the water.

Born underwater, hippo babies swim before they learn to walk. Until old enough to fend for itself, each barrel-bodied youngster cruises aboard its mother's back.

Young and old alike need water to protect their tough but sensitive skin from the searing African sun. Although hippo hides are thick enough to stand the ravages of hunters' spears and rivals' teeth, drying opens painful-looking cracks.

Sometimes a pinkish, oily fluid oozes from the skin, apparently to help keep it moist.

A cooling rain may bring hippos ashore to graze in daylight, but they usually wait for the sun to set. Then they leave the water to browse among juicy grasses—sometimes wandering miles in the process. It takes five or six bushels of grass to stuff a grownup hippo's stomach.

In today's Africa, hunters have wiped out the hippo inhabitants of some areas, reducing the creatures' territory to the central and southern regions of the continent.

But, happily, Africa is a big place. There still are plenty of spots where a hippo can throw its weight around.

395 words

4

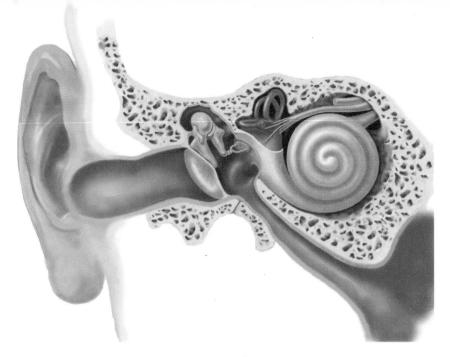

The Incredible Ear

Note these words:
hydraulic pressure (hī·drô′lĭk): *pressure of
a liquid in motion*
staccato (stə·kät′ō): *abrupt*

The human ear is a mysterious structure which scientists are just beginning to understand. We have known for a long time about the way sound travels through the ear, but we are just now learning how we hear. The best theories of hearing are only partial explanations. The ear is an engineering marvel and its range of sounds is amazing.

An engineer would have virtually an impossible task if he tried to duplicate the ear's miniaturization. To do it, the engineer would have to cram into a cubic inch of space an automated, sophisticated sound system. It would require specialized equipment not found in the best-equipped sound studio. And still, the engineer with his equipment would not be able to match the ear's performance.

As a machine, the ear is able to multiply forces applied to it as much as 90 times. The mechanical forces applied by sound waves on the eardrum are multiplied by a lever system consisting of three small bones. This amplified mechanical force is changed into hydraulic pressure within the inner ear. There the hydraulic pressure is converted into electrical energy which travels as an electrical impulse to the brain. It is in the brain that actual hearing takes place.

Loud noises which beat with large forces on the eardrum can cause damage to our ears and impair hearing. Fortunately, most ordinary loud noises are not multiplied by the lever system. The ear automatically adjusts itself to dampen the effects of such large forces. Unexpected loud noises, however, do sometimes cause damage.

The range of the human ear is incredible. The ear can hear sounds so weak that they vibrate the eardrum with a movement that is less than the width of a hydrogen molecule. On the other hand, most strong sounds that hammer viciously on the eardrum do the ear no harm. We can hear both a whisper and the harsh staccato noise of a machine gun.

Scientists tell us that a normal person can distinguish more than 400,000 sounds. Some African tribesmen have ears so sensitive that they can hear the slightest murmur across a clearing the size of a football field.

The full range and capacity of our ears is not yet known. But God knows the capacity of our ears because He designed them. It was God who designed the ear as a delicate but efficient machine. It was God who set in motion the forces of the universe and established the forces of sound waves.

415 words

6

Nature's Sandpiles

Note this word:

caroming: *colliding and bouncing back*

Dunes are nature's sandpiles, play-things of the wind. A steady breeze can keep a mountainous dune on the move forever.

But, if you go out dune-watching, don't expect any great excitement. The huge piles of sand move only about 20 feet a year—about two-thirds of an inch a day.

Once I spent several hours watching a dune move. I almost needed a magnifying glass. There was only one spot near the center of the mammoth crescent where I could detect any action at all. Then I discovered an amazing, yet simple, thing—dunes move not as a body but one little grain at a time.

Naturally, wind can't push along an entire dune. It must be done grain by grain, a caroming effect as in marbles. Normally, a sand grain is not lifted into the air by wind. It is bounced. One grain hits another, causing it to ricochet and hit others. Soon the air is filled with hopping, bobbing grains of sand. But even when the wind is strongest, a single bit of sand in a dune rarely travels more than three or four feet.

There are five general types of dunes: beach dunes; wavelike ridges that form in deserts at a right angle to the wind; longitudinal sand dunes that parallel the wind's direction; U-shaped dunes whose open ends face windward; and barchans, the photographically ideal lunar crescents whose horns point downwind.

The Great Sand Dunes in Colorado cover 27 square miles and are steadily marching with the wind, smothering grass, trees, and even a small stream.

Coastal dunes in Europe and eastern United States have likewise covered nearby farms and woods. A small village on Germany's Baltic coast was slowly buried during a 30-year span, then quietly uncovered in the next 30 years.

But man has recently learned that coastal dunes have a definite purpose in nature's scheme—protection of shorelines from pounding seas. Massachusetts law prohibits any tampering with dunes.

On North Carolina's Outer Banks, the world's most famous dune—Kill Devil Hill—has ceased to be one. While the Wright Brothers were experimenting with their air machine, Kill Devil Hill was marching steadily southward at about 20 feet a year. In 1929, it was permanently rooted by planting grass on its graceful slopes.

Not all dunes travel. In Africa's Sahara, some seem not to have moved in the memory of man. Also, dunes and deserts do not always go together. Only a ninth of the Sahara's 3,500,000 square miles wears golden, sharply crested dunes.

430 words STOP

8

Raindrop Miracles

It has always seemed to me that the rainbow is one of God's most beautiful and fascinating creations, but when someone explained to me what a rainbow really is, I began to see it as nothing short of a miracle.

As one would guess, a rainbow is caused by the effect of sun shining on rain. When the sun peeks out from between the clouds after a shower, the rainbow appears in the sky opposite the sun.

We can usually see three or four distinct colors in the rainbow. However, scientists and careful observers tell me that there are actually six colors—red, orange, yellow, green, blue, and violet. Did you know that the sunshine itself is made up of these six colors, each color with its own wave length?

You may know that when sunlight enters a prism, the light is bent or refracted and changed into its six colors. The same thing happens when sunlight enters a raindrop. The drop of water acts as a tiny prism. The light is refracted and divided into the six colors. After that, the sun rays are reflected and scattered. If there are enough raindrops for prisms, we see a gorgeous rainbow!

It is especially interesting to know that as we view a rainbow we are actually seeing a series of rainbows because of the constant flow of rain. The rainbow is indeed a beautiful moving picture! Raindrops are curved; thus rainbows are curved.

You have probably seen what appeared to be a little rainbow when viewing the sun shining in the lawn sprinkler. The same principles apply to form that rainbow as the one you see in the sky. The colors result from the sun shining on the raindrops which in turn act as small prisms. Because the raindrops you see from a waterfall or sprinkler are very small, the rainbow you see appears to be very light. The colors are quite dim and appear to fade into each other.

Raindrops must be large for a large and brilliant rainbow. The larger the raindrops, the more brilliant the rainbow. Why? Because these raindrops act as prisms to cause refraction of the sun's rays. This is why snowflakes cannot cause rainbows; they are too dense for sunlight to pass through. If you have heard of someone who thought he saw a rainbow when snow was falling, it was only because the snow was mixed with rain.

The next time you see a rainbow, think of how God causes little raindrops to make the miracle of the rainbow.

430 words STOP

Mollusk Mansions

Note these words:
conch (kŏngk)
whorls (hwôrlz): *spirals*
gastropods: *type of mollusk*
operculum (ō·pər′kū·ləm)

When I was small, a visiting relative brought me a conch shell from Florida. Our whole family admired its smooth-as-glass pink lip, the perfect whorls on the end, and the sound of waves when you held it to your ear.

What a surprise when I later met the builder of this wonder! The live conch turned out to be a dark, wet-looking thing that poked beady eyes out of its sunrise-tinted shell.

As I grew older and learned more about nature, I realized the conch was not an exception but a rule. Earth's shell-building animals create some of the loveliest forms found anywhere. But the creatures called mollusks, who build with such delicacy, often are drab-colored blobs.

Mollusks take their name from a Latin word *molluscus,* meaning "soft." The mollusk's simple body lacks a skeleton to give it shape. So it builds a case, at once its external skeleton, its house, and its fortress.

The building tool of this master mason is its mantle, a muscular fold of flesh that covers the animal's back and sides. Pores in the mantle ooze a calcium-rich liquid that hardens into shell. To "paint" its house with colorful patterns, the mollusk's body makes pigments out of chemicals in its environment.

Many mollusks glide in and out of their homes, but the animals remain firmly attached to the shells. They add onto the shell edges as they grow and repair any damage.

Mollusk mansions take many forms. Each species has a favorite building style. Some construct simple cap-shaped shells. Others make curved tubes that resemble elephant tusks. Some, like knights of old, cover themselves with eight curved plates of shell armor.

Bivalves, such as clams and oysters, live within a hinged pair of look-alike trapdoors. Gastropods like the conch spend their lives going in circles. They start with a tiny twist of shell and keep growing, building, and spiraling round and round. Some add a trapdoor entrance called an operculum for extra security.

Taken all together, the mollusks number about 70,000 living species.

Through ages, men have gathered the empty shell houses to make jewelry, use as money, or just admire. The purple dye that colored Roman emperors' robes came from a gastropod.

Serious collectors called conchologists may pay thousands of dollars for a single rare specimen. But to me the value of a shell cannot be measured in dollars. It must be measured in the eyes of a child when he first learns that even a lowly snail or sea worm can build a palace fit for a king.

STOP

435 words

Up and Away in a Hot-Air Balloon

Richard M. Crum

"A huge nylon bag, filled with hot air, pulls me skyward.

"I'm soaring 3,000 feet above the ground. Suddenly I hear someone call, 'Please, mister, won't you get me down?'

"Somehow the balloon's ground line has wrapped around a boy's hand, and I have unwittingly lifted him up with me!

"As quickly as I can, I descend, talking to the boy quietly, telling him to watch me, not the ground. Finally, two miles from our takeoff point, 11-year-old Danny Nowell hits the earth—a little hard, and terribly frightened, but miraculously unscathed."

Thus William Berry, a California businessman, recalls his most harrowing ascent in the sport of hot-air ballooning.

Mr. Berry's unwilling passenger was not the first boy to tangle with a balloon. In 1843, a French youngster was snagged by the anchor of a runaway hot-air balloon.

Since man's first conquest of the air, boys have found it

hard to stay away from balloons. In fact, the dawn of flight in the United States involves a 13-year-old lad.

Young Edward Warren watched excitedly that day in 1784. Peter Carnes, the first American to make and launch a balloon, was publicly demonstrating his air globe in Baltimore, Maryland.

So thrilled by the magic of flight was Edward that he volunteered to go up. The hot-air bag, secured by a tether, carried the boy aloft, and Edward became the first person in the United States to ascend in a balloon. The adventure took place less than a year after a hot-air balloon lifted two Frenchmen above Paris rooftops on history's first manned aerial voyage. Their craft was designed by Joseph and Jacques Étienne Montgolfier, the Wright brothers of ballooning.

Balloonists apply the simple fact that hot air rises. Today, bottled-gas burners mounted above the gondola—where the pilot rides—heat the air in the bag. Increase the flame, the balloon rises. Decrease it, the balloon descends.

Without helm or rudder, a balloonist can travel only where wind currents take him.

Since 1960, the rediscovery of hot-air ballooning as a sport has triggered the growth of ballooning clubs in the United States. "It's the quiet that appeals to me most in ballooning," says Mr. Berry. "The quiet, and the sense of freedom, and the challenge."

Bringing a balloon back to earth safely requires wide-open spaces, one reason the sport centers in the western United States.

Where a balloonist lands depends greatly on the whim of the wind. "I've landed in water and among trees," says Mr. Berry. "And once I landed right next to a lion pit in a zoo."

STOP
450 words

Summer Ice Storms

Hail hurts. The rock-hard pellets of ice hurtle from the sky with brutal force. The only way to escape them is to hold your arms over your head and race for cover. Curling up in a ditch offers fair protection against lightning when there is no other shelter, but you're in for a bruising beating if the thunderstorm holds hail.

Hail hurts in another way. I once saw valuable crops shredded as if by giant claws in a hailstorm only a few minutes long. Annual crop losses in North Carolina alone average above a million dollars. Especially cruel storms have so damaged fields that farmers had to fold up and move to city jobs.

Because the hail season hits its peak just as the wheat crop reaches maturity, Kansas suffers more hail damage than any other state. The crop-damage total is ten times greater than the state's average tornado loss.

Hail forms when ice builds around a nucleus—a bit of dust or a snow-like speck of moisture. It forms in clouds one or two miles above the earth, usually in the leading edge of storms where winds blow hardest. Layer upon layer of ice forms when the nucleus collides with super-cooled water— water that remains liquid below the freezing point. Each collision adds a new layer of ice. At last the hailstone—for that is what it has become—gets too heavy for the high-altitude winds to support it, and it plummets to earth.

Of course, there is not just one stone in a hailstorm, but many.

A suburb of Denver, Colorado, reeled under a storm that left a layer of hailstones four to six inches deep. Wind and a raging downpour on the heels of an 1890 Iowa hailstorm piled icy drifts six feet deep.

Hailstones range from pea-size upward through egg- and baseball-size. The largest on record was a monster a pound and a half heavy and 17 inches around. The giant fell on Potter, Nebraska, in 1928.

Though there are spots where hail rarely falls, no place is entirely safe. Even the faraway Fiji Islands in the South Pacific record an occasional hailstorm. In the United States, hailstorms are few and far between in much of Florida, but fairly frequent around Denver, Colorado, and in Cheyenne, Wyoming.

Damage from hail to crops, cars, and buildings reaches millions of dollars every year. In its own way, the icy terror of a hailstorm is as awful as a tornado.

Still, there is something exciting about a hailstorm. I always discover a fresh feeling of wonder when nature drops ice on my doorstep at the height of a warm-weather storm.

455 words STOP

The Pincushion

The porcupine is not a large animal, but he is feared by some of the biggest. Even a tiger will think twice before tangling with this two-foot-long terror.

Most of the time this prickly pincushion merely minds his own business. However, if something wants to start trouble, "Porky" will give it a fight.

From his neck to his tail is a heavy coat of quills. They look like someone's knitting needles. Each quill is sharp and painful if it sticks you.

Porcupines appear to be slow and helpless. Yet, if you attack one, he will turn quickly and try to back into you. He does it so fast that he will probably get his attacker. Sometimes dogs will run at a porcupine, expecting an easy dinner. Porky will turn, lift his tail, and push his back at the rushing dog. The quills will stick into the dog's face and come loose from the porcupine. The dog limps away with a painful howl. Some quills are 15 inches long and sink deeply into the skin.

A few stories about porcupines aren't true. They can't really shoot their quills like arrows. However, they can push their body fast enough to cause serious injury.

Porcupines have 30,000 quills on their back and sides. Don't try to count them or they might give a few to you. But that would be no problem since he would quickly grow them back.

A quill is not merely a sharp stick. Each quill has tiny blades all over it. After it goes inside an animal, the quill will push itself deeper and deeper even after it has left the porcupine. The result is often a nasty wound.

Mountain lions can successfully hunt porcupines, but even they have to be careful. Only the head or belly can be attacked. Carefully and quickly the lion has to roll the porcupine on its back.

If a coyote attacks a porcupine, he may get killed. He jumps at the animal and gets a face full of quills. The quills then begin to work their way into the coyote's throat and head. It won't take too long before the wounded attacker is dead.

Usually the animal which gets hurt by a porcupine is the one who doesn't look at the danger. It doesn't realize or care what the Porky can do. It just rushes in and comes away the loser.

We often do the same thing. "Why not just try some foolish thing? What does it matter if we get into trouble?" Because we didn't stop to think, we end up in more trouble than we ever imagined. A smart person stops to think it over. When he realizes the harm, he decides against trouble.

455 words

Beaver Business

Chiseltooth is my kind of critter. Even though beavers are rodents, relatives of the rat, in my book they are forest gentlefolk.

They mind their own business, too, which is whittling trees into hourglass shapes and making logs that look like sharpened pencils. The cutting tools are big buckteeth that grow constantly. Beavers must gnaw just to wear down their incisors.

I've never seen an eager beaver. The wood-eaters I've observed seemed a little lazy; but they are persistent. These engineers keep plugging away.

Their dams have an underwater base of mud and stones. Projecting logs, poles, and branches are anchored in the bottom of the stream. Some of their dams are 1,000 feet long. Where many beavers work, a kind of woodsy Netherlands appears, complete with dikes and canals.

Soon, ponds and lakes brim behind dams of mud, boughs, and stones. Fish flourish here. Migrating birds alight. Wild creatures congregate.

The way I see it, beavers do more for the environment than most of us. Untamed nature can be pretty rough sometimes. To help smooth things over, these furry conservationists cut down erosion

19

and raise water tables by slowing runoff.

The first time I encountered a beaver, I was canoeing on the Connecticut River in New Hampshire. So was the beaver. Actually, the beaver's canoe-paddle tail is used more for building than rowing.

Fussy little fellow, this Yankee beaver. Slapped his tail on the water as if to tell me to move on. I did, but returned at twilight.

I sat on a rock. The beaver patrolled. Then, becoming used to my presence, he paused for a snack, stripping twigs and bark from a branch. The nearby lodge, a big mound of mud and branches, lay half in the water and half on the bank.

Back in 1808, the story goes, a trapper and explorer named John Colter was chased by Blackfoot Indians out in Yellowstone country. Thinking fast, he dived into a stream and supposedly swam into a submerged beaver tunnel. It led to a dry, warm lodge where he hid until the Indians went away.

Colter was lucky. The home folks were out. Though beavers would rather swim than fight, it wouldn't be too healthy to corner a bigtooth family in their dark den. There beavers snooze away the wintertime, waiting out the cold. For food they simply munch twigs from the lodge's ceiling and walls.

Explorers found North America alive with beavers. Needless to say the trappers made a killing. The breed thinned out fast, but today beavers are making a comeback with man's help. Some have been parachuted into remote areas as part of conservation schemes. I've even seen a beaver lodge on national parkland near Washington, D.C., just a fifteen-minute drive from the White House.

470 words

The Valiant Horse

When the dust from the Battle of the Little Bighorn had cleared, cavalrymen found the sole survivor. He stood, head bowed, above the bodies of the dead soldiers. He was pierced with arrows and bullets. Blood oozed from many wounds. He was an Army horse named Comanche.

Custer's disastrous last stand marked Comanche's last battle. The veteran war horse spent his remaining 15 years in retirement.

Comanche was one of a noble parade of horses that have helped fight men's battles from ancient through modern times. Alexander the Great had a favorite steed named Bucephalus [byōō·sĕf′ə·ləs]. Still a boy, Alexander tamed the fiery stallion, and Bucephalus would tolerate no other rider.

Alexander treated his horse with affection and understanding. In the horse's later years, Alexander usually used another mount for preliminary maneuvering, saving Bucephalus' strength for crucial combat. When the steed died during a battle in the Punjab region of what is now Pakistan, Alexander founded a town in honor of his beloved charger.

Gen. Robert E. Lee's Traveller is one of the best-known military mounts. When both rider and mount had retired, Lee proudly recounted how his "Confederate gray horse" had never once faltered.

Horses served the Union cause, too. Confederate troops were harassing Gen. Philip Sheridan's troops while the general was some 20 miles away, at Winchester, Virginia. To inspire his men and help save the day, Sheridan needed fast transportation—which his coal-black steed provided. The horse hero, formerly called Rienzi after the Mississippi town where he was presented to Sheridan, was rechristened Winchester. His trip was celebrated in "Sheridan's Ride" by Thomas Buchanan Read:

> *. . . And when their statues*
>   *are placed on high . . .*
> *Be it said in letters both*
>   *bold and bright:*
> *'Here is the steed that*
>   *saved the day*
> *By carrying Sheridan*
>   *into the fight,*
> *From Winchester—*
>   *20 miles away!'*

The last great cavalry charge on record took place during World War II. An Italian cavalry battalion, trapped by a superior Soviet force, charged to cover a retreat. Later, Italian soldiers found Albino, the sole surviving horse, minus one eye and with a bullet through his leg. He recovered and returned to Italy, but in the confusion following the war was sold. The commander searched the country for Albino and finally spied him pulling a vegetable cart. Pensioned for life by the Italian Government, Albino died a peaceful death in 1960.

Reckless, a Korean mare, played a valiant role in the Korean conflict of the early 1950's by serving as ammunition carrier for a U.S. Marine platoon. She was decorated for bravery and made an honorary sergeant.

Today, military horses have largely ceremonial duties, serving as symbols of valiant deeds and dead heroes. One, named Black Jack, marched riderless in the funeral of President John F. Kennedy. Still active at 25, he was honored each year at a birthday party. One attentive fan even provided a birthday cake in Black Jack's favorite flavor: butter pecan.

490 words

Michigan's Magic Island

Patricia F. Robbins

Most people seek out an island retreat because of something it has. But people come to Michigan's Mackinac Island because of something it *doesn't* have—automobiles.

On Mackinac (pronounced MACK-uh-naw to rhyme with hack 'n' saw) there are no cars. Not even any motorbikes. Just the jingle of plain old bicycle bells and the clop of horses' hooves.

Policemen ride bikes and horses. A local bank provides a "trot-in" window. And on hot days harried city dwellers stream off ferries from the Michigan mainland and gently ease themselves backward in time.

Tiny Mackinac Island—just two miles wide, three miles long, and nine miles around the edge—has 25 miles of drives, bridle paths, and foot-paths that wind along a sandy shore, through cool pine forests, and over the island's rock-ribbed midsection. Visitors can go back a century to the tranquil Main Street of small-town America or many centuries to Indian campfires. There legends grew about spirits who lived in the island's unusual rock formations—formations with names like Arch Rock, Sugar Loaf, and Devil's Kitchen.

Mackinac Island looks peaceful today, but once it rang with war whoops, gunfire, and the noisy laughter of fur trappers swapping pelts and tall tales. Its location made Mackinac a natural stopping place for men traveling through the Great Lakes. It sits astride the Straits of Mackinac where Lake Huron meets Lake Michigan. Here the Upper and Lower Michigan Peninsulas almost touch.

Indians paddled their canoes to the island centuries ago to fish, to escape enemies, and to bury dead chieftains among the great spirits. They called the spot Michilimackinac.

Jesuit missionaries arrived in the 1600's with European ideas and with European lilacs that still tint the island purple each June.

Because so many French fur traders stopped regularly at the island, French soldiers built a mainland fort nearby to protect them. After the French and Indian War, victorious British took over the fort and built a new one on the island itself overlooking the harbor. Much of the fort still stands today.

But it was fur, not firearms, that really put Mackinac on the map. The American millionaire John Jacob Astor made the island trading post the headquarters of his far-flung American Fur Company in the early part of the 19th century. During 1822—a peak year—thousands of traders swarmed to Mackinac during the summer to sell or barter $3,000,000 worth of pelts.

Fur trade declined after the mid-1800's, but summer traffic kept on growing. Rich businessmen built vacation homes. The Grand Hotel, opened in 1887, rolled out 30,000 square yards of red carpet for guests and lined an 880-foot front porch with rockers—a must for resort hotels at the turn of the century.

To keep this gentle Victorian flavor, Mackinac residents banned the noisy invention called the motorcar. No one seems to miss it. Today more than half a million visitors jounce, pedal, and tramp around the island each summer, enjoying what one 19th-century writer called its "refreshing and inspiring landscape."

510 words

STOP

25

The Windmill: Energy's Friend

I recall a summer long past when the wind refused to blow across north Texas. The windmill wouldn't turn, and the water hid deep in the earth.

Each day we got drier. We young people took to washing our hands in sand to help out a little.

One sunset the clouds hung limp, like sails of becalmed ships. After moonrise the windmill looked like an erect old lady with a round poke bonnet on her head. Did I hear right? The bonnet was creaking. A thin breeze turned the fan around once. The wind thickened, and the blades whirled, and soon we heard that wondrous sound of water pouring into the tank. Yipee! We lived again.

I'll never forget those fine old Texas ladies in their bonnets, standing tall like masted schooners catching the tides of the air.

Today windmills are called "near-perfect ecological machines," now that they are almost gone, now that nostalgia has set in. But it's no sentimental tale that they work in harmony with the earth.

Many easterners buy one just to own a bit of the past. A mill costs little to maintain and the fuel's as free as the breeze. Such economy impresses foreign farmers. Windmills now turn in lands as far apart as India, Australia, and Argentina.

In our own land, between 1880 and 1935, six and a half million windmills were erected. "The vast prairie land is fairly alive with them," a visitor to Kansas said 75 years ago. Then the wind pumped water, sawed wood, and ran cream separators. Electricity arrived on the prairie in the 1930's and banished millions of hardworking windmills from the American scene.

Today most of the fan wheels are gone, and TV antennas stand atop the moldering skeletons of neglected windmill pylons. Maybe it takes such a death to bring about a rebirth.

Some U.S. energy experts say windmills, even perched atop skyscrapers, could help ease the nation's power pinch. Mechanical engineers look back longingly to a magnificent experiment along these lines. I'm proud our country made the world's biggest, most powerful windmill.

Built like a sleek aircraft, this supercharged monster had two metal wings designed like airscrews. They swiveled to catch the wind. They glinted from Grandpa Knob near Rutland, Vermont. The turbine measured 150 feet across. During World War II it tamed winds up to 70 miles an hour and turned the force into commercial electrical energy. But the great windmill threw a blade and the project was abandoned.

All of us are entitled to dreams now and then. One of mine is to see windmills turning again, bustling in the breeze, doing useful work, and helping save fuel resources.

The mills, equipped with electric alternators, would serve Space Age homesteaders. The pioneers could redeem our worn-out lands. They might need a boost from rooftop sunpower, too. Big central power stations need not do all the work. Small energy converters—not quite as small as a squirrel—can give us valuable energy bonus.

To a wanderer like me the sun and the wind are old friends. I think if people used these natural forces, life could be better. It's worth a try.

535 words STOP

The Unchanging Bible and Science

True science and the Bible never conflict. But the Bible and **unproven scientific theories** always conflict. The Bible stands firm and unchanging while the theories of science change constantly. To change is the very nature of science and, as facts are discovered, science slowly comes to agree with the Bible. To see how science agrees with the Bible, look at a few of the many scientific facts stated in the Bible. At first these facts were rejected by science, but now they have been accepted to be correct.

Solomon wrote almost 1,000 years before Christ was born that the earth is a circle (Prov. 8:27). The word used for *circle* by Solomon means "spherical." At that time all civilizations except Israel considered the earth to be flat. The earliest record that anyone other than God's people believed the earth to be a sphere is found in Aristotle's writings. He lived three hundred years before Christ. It was not until the 1400s that scientists accepted the idea of a spherical earth, although many people rejected the idea. It was not until the twentieth century that the earth was proved to be a sphere.

Moses wrote the book of Genesis more than 1,400 years before Christ was born. In the first chapter he writes about "the firmament of the heaven" (Gen. 1:14–18). The word *firmament* means a "spreading out expanse." In other words, Moses was saying that the universe is expanding. Today, astronomers tell us this is so. But until the 1900s scientists thought the universe was limited in size. In fact, the idea of an expanding universe was not proved until about 1950.

About six centuries before Christ was born, Jeremiah wrote that the stars cannot be numbered (Jer. 33:22). Scientists, on the other hand, just 150 years before the birth of Christ claimed there were only 3,000 stars. Galileo in A.D. 1608 first used a telescope to study the heavens and discovered a vast multitude of stars that had never before been seen. He concluded that the stars are indeed innumerable. Today we know that our galaxy, which contains unknown billions of stars, is just one galaxy among billions, and astronomers tell us that each galaxy contains billions of stars. Modern astronomers conclude that we cannot determine the number of the stars.

Fifteen to twenty centuries before Christ was born, Job wrote that ". . . the morning stars sang together" (Job 38:7). In the oldest book of the Bible, God declares through a humble man that the stars give off sound. During World War II, U.S. Army scientists first heard the stars. At that time, they had no idea that they were hearing sound from a star. By accident, they had picked up sound generated by sun spots. Today, with their radio telescopes, astronomers receive and analyze sound from stars that are too distant to be seen by the strongest optical telescope.

Yes, the Bible is without doubt scientifically accurate. Because God is its author, we can depend upon it to be true, accurate, and unchanging. But we must realize that science is not always accurate and that it is always changing. After all, science is based on man's very limited understanding of God's marvelous creation.

540 words STOP

The Blossoming Tulip Business

Tulips are as Dutch as windmills and wooden shoes. But it's mainly the bulbs, not the blossoms, that the world buys from the Netherlands. All those square miles of brilliant spring flowers are a blooming nuisance to Dutch tulip farmers.

Left on the stalk, flowers draw strength from the bulbs. To produce fat bulbs bursting with flower power, cultivators must behead each slender plant.

For one flower the work is a snap. Multiply the effort by billions, and you have backaches by the thousands for Dutch field hands. It's one big headache for the tulip farm owner, too.

Mountains of blossoms must be disposed of. Youngsters get out of bed before dawn to buy wheelbarrow loads of tulip blooms. They fashion bright necklaces for the crowds of foreign visitors who attend the Netherlands' flower outburst each April or early May. North Sea cold keeps Dutch tulip time four to five weeks behind the blossom season in most of the United States.

Flower farm visitors view the color extravaganza from a safe distance. The Dutch workmen themselves literally tiptoe through the tulips to avoid crushing any foliage. Breaks could provide starting places for infectious plant diseases.

When the field of tulip greens withers, farmers harvest the buried crop. Heavy, export-size bulbs soak in hot-water vats. Careful doses of wet heat kill harmful eel worms, cleanse away dirt, and help produce colossal blooms. Dry-heat treatment toughens bulbs for travel.

Small bulblets go back into the soil for more growing time. After about three years they become large enough to throw their weight around in international tulip trade.

The bulb itself is a little plant wrapped up in protective layers of plant food and containing a triggering mechanism. It's a floral time bomb. Flower farmers know that a period of cold is required to wind up the plant's biological clock. There is no problem when bulbs travel to areas with freezing winters. But people from the tropics order tulips, too, and expect them to bloom.

Dutchmen chill bulbs destined for southern regions of the United States and for warm countries. For lands of the Southern Hemisphere—where July is midwinter—bulbs are held over in cold storage. A special tulip research laboratory in the Netherlands works out tables of cold-storage times. Bulbs are shipped to arrive in places like Australia, New Zealand, and Argentina at the proper time for fall planting and spring blooming.

The Japanese work hard to break into the international bulb market, but Dutchmen hold the lead. They have been gaining experience for centuries. The first tulips arrived in Europe from Turkey in the 1550s.

By 1634 the Dutch were caught up in a frenzy of buying and selling the fashionable flowers in operations similar to those of a stock market. Bulb fanciers bid up the prices to as high as $10,000. Historians call it "tulipomania."

A sailor fresh from a journey spied a tulip bulb on a merchant's desk. Thinking it was a scrawny onion, he ate it with his raw herring for lunch. The meal was worth $1,400 and cost the sailor five months in jail.

When the bubble burst on February 3, 1636, many Dutchmen lost fortunes before they regained their senses. Strict rules governing the industry grew out of the crash and put bulb growing on a businesslike basis.

STOP

560 words

33

Homing Pigeon Heroes

Every time I cross unfamiliar ground with the help of my battered old compass, I marvel at the birds called homing pigeons. They can zoom back to their lofts from more than 1,000 miles away. And no one knows exactly how they do it.

For centuries humans have used the bird's remarkable instinct to provide fast communication. Some think Noah had the idea first. The Bible says he released a dove after the flood and it returned with an olive twig. But bird fanciers insist a dove doesn't "home"; it must have been a pigeon.

Pigeon or dove—it's all in the family Columbidae, which numbers nearly 300 species. As early as 3000 B.C., Egyptians began to breed special strains for use as messengers. Pigeons sped names of Olympic winners to towns in ancient Greece. The Sultan of Baghdad linked his empire with a pigeon-post system in 1150.

Seven centuries later, message-carrying pigeons started Paul Julius Reuter on his way to founding a global news service. And more recently a modern newsman had his photofilm of a moon shot airlifted to the office by a homing pigeon.

Pigeons have served armies since the days when Caesar conquered Gaul. Microphotography—the science of making tiny pictures—added to the birds' usefulness. A single pigeon could carry 40,000 microfilmed dispatches. Thousands of birds served during both world wars. Some earned medals for winning battles or saving lives. One named G. I. Joe flew 20 miles in 20 minutes.

Today most pigeons fly just for sport. Organized racing began in Belgium in the early 1800s and soon spread. Fanciers breed and race their own birds. Even Queen Elizabeth of England has had her own pigeon loft.

Training begins when birds are about four weeks old. First they sit on the loft. Then they "roam" on their own nearby. Finally owners take them on longer and longer trips.

In races, specially banded birds are taken in crates to the starting point and liberated. When each bird comes home, its owner removes the band and inserts it into a device that records the time. Distance from starting point to loft is measured; times are checked; and the bird that made it home fastest wins.

Opinions vary on how homers do their special thing. Some say they sight by the sun or use the earth's magnetism as a compass. But for every theory there's some contrary evidence. Researchers have reported birds that could home in spite of clouds, blindfolds, artificial changes in day and night, and disruption of the normal magnetic field.

Whatever gives pigeons their sense of direction, it sometimes fails. Lost birds have turned up months or years after a race, continents away from home. Strong wind, fog, and possibly even TV signals may throw the birds off course.

When all goes well, a homer can clip along at 35 to 70 miles an hour. With the right wind, birds have been clocked as fast as 90 miles an hour. Flights of more than a thousand miles are common for mature racers, and one U.S. Army pigeon made a 2,300-mile flight.

So strong is the homing instinct, birds will hoof it if they must. A South African farmer told of selling five pigeons to a neighbor a mile away. He plucked some feathers so they couldn't fly back. But they came home anyway—bedraggled from the hike.

570 words STOP

The Real Scoop about Ice Cream

"Come right on in," Dr. Wendell Arbuckle welcomed me. "I'm just sampling a batch of rhubarb ice cream we made fresh this morning."

I eagerly volunteered to lend Dr. Arbuckle a hand—or a taste bud—in what must be one of the sweetest and coolest jobs in the world. He is Professor of Dairy Manufacturing at the University of Maryland, specializing in ice cream.

"I worked on this one a long time," he said, handing me a spoonful of the creamy, pale-pink concoction, "trying to bring out the flavor of fresh rhubarb. I think I finally found the secret—a dash of mace and a hint of preserved orange rind."

Whatever the ingredients, I pronounced it delicious. Smiling at my unscientific approach, Dr. Arbuckle showed me the scorecard his students use to rate their products.

"Really good ice cream we rate 'mellow,'" he explained. "Not only does the flavor have to be just right, but the texture should be smooth and what we term 'medium-resistant.' A lot depends on keeping the ice crystals just the right size."

A rather shy, modest man, Dr. Arbuckle didn't have to tell me what I already knew—that he did much of the pioneering work probing the internal structure of ice cream. To non-scientific ice-cream eaters he is better known for such flavorful inventions as sweet potato ice cream, introduced at the 1964 New York World's Fair.

An earlier world's fair—held in St. Louis, Missouri, in 1904—probably saw the debut of the ice-cream cone. This seemingly all-American institution was an on-the-spot invention by a Syrian named Ernest Hanwi who had emigrated to St. Louis the year before. He had a stand at the fair where he sold *zalabia,* a crisp, wafer-thin waffle popular in the Middle East. One day when the ice-cream concession next to Hanwi's stand ran out of dishes, he came to the rescue by rolling his waffles into cones.

Serendipity—or happy accident—plays a large role in the story of ice cream. The world's first wholesale ice-cream factory was opened in Baltimore, Maryland, in 1851 by a milk dealer who had a large surplus of cream. Ice-cream sodas were the hasty invention of Robert Green, who was demonstrating a soda fountain at an exposition in Philadelphia. To show prospective buyers how the fountain worked, Green was making a soda popular at that time—a mixture of syrup, carbonated water, and cream. When he ran out of cream, he substituted ice cream and created the classic soda-fountain standby.

When I asked Dr. Arbuckle if there were any recent innovations, he disappeared into the freezer and emerged with a couple of grape-ice pops.

"These are made with whey," he announced as we sampled the Popsicles. "When you make cheese," he explained, "the watery substance left after you separate out the curd is called whey. Little Miss Muffet ate it, but now it usually gets thrown out. If you substitute whey for the water generally used to make ice pops, it doesn't change the taste but it makes them more nourishing."

Eating the nutritious and delicious Popsicle, I felt grateful to ice-cream innovators, from the serendipitous Mr. Hanwi to the scientific Dr. Arbuckle. Thanks to them, we have a treat that's hard to beat but easy to lick.

570 words

Squid Tricks

Patricia F. Robbins

What changes color, shape, and direction in a flash, carries its own disguise kit, and comes in lengths that range from minnow to whale?

Give up? Try the versatile squid, one of nature's wonders.

Squids (that's right—one *squid,* two *squids*) range from dime-size to 60 feet or even longer. Hundreds of species display a bewildering array of colors and characteristics. Some jet along at speeds that rival the fastest game fish; others just drift. Some content themselves with bits of plant life; others will attack anything that looks edible, even a whale.

The squid's shy habits make it a much misunderstood mollusk. Scientists get little chance to study it at close range. Trapped in a tank, the high-strung creature will dart, squirt, and leap erratically until it dies of shock, days or even minutes later.

A few large members of the family give the whole clan a bad press. Sailors who sighted the giant *Architeuthis* told tales of a monster that dragged men and ships to watery graves. And almost everyone has bitten fingernails reading about the diver battling writhing octopus or squid tentacles.

No wonder many people consider squids ugly, unpleasant creatures. Actually they are marvels of construction—adaptable, intelligent, and often quite beautiful.

Squids belong to the group of soft-bodied boneless animals called mollusks. The class name, *Cephalopoda,* comes from Greek words meaning head and foot.

At first glance, cephalopods [sef′ə·lə·pädz′]—squids, octopuses, and cuttlefishes—do seem to be all head and foot. Or rather, head and feet.

A squid's feet, usually called arms, bunch at one end of its head-and-body combination. The cluster includes two long arms called tentacles, plus eight smaller arms. Little suction cups tip the tentacles and line the arms to help the squid get a good grip on dinner.

Squids spot dinner—which can be most anything in the sea—with two complicated eyes much like the eyes of a man. Scientists consider squids the most intelligent mollusks.

Swimming along they look like submarines. Usually they move backward, propelling themselves by squirting water out of a nozzle near their heads. To change direction they don't even have to turn their bodies. They just flip the nozzle and shift into instant reverse.

In time of crisis, a squid jets off with a great blast of water, leaving behind a squirt of ink. The ink forms a squidlike shape and sometimes fools the enemy.

To speed its getaway, the squid slips on a disguise by turning a different color. Little sacs of pigment dot the mantle, or body covering. By using muscles to open and close different sacs, squids can turn a variety of shades.

Some species also produce their own underwater psychedelic shows. Built-in light organs called photophores create colored light by chemical reaction, the same way a firefly does.

Squids specialize in split-second change. They have to. Nearly every other sea creature considers the squid a taste treat, and many men agree. Squids feed more people than any other sea animals except fish. Cooks in Europe and the Far East fry, curry, marinate, sauté, stew, and stuff them.

Most Americans scorn squid as a main dish, but fishermen off the coasts of California and Newfoundland haul in tons each year to sell as fish bait. They catch the squids with bright, cigar-shaped lures called jiggers.

Now scientists seek out squids to learn the secrets of their speed and adaptability. One secret may be a supersize nervous system. Squid nerves contain huge fibers—up to 100 times the size of man's. This gives squids the largest internal signal system in the animal kingdom. By studying it, biologists hope to learn more about man's network of nerves.

After all, cephalopods swim in all the world's oceans. They must be doing something right.

640 words STOP

Riding the Rapids
Charles B. Cramer

Take a bunch of summer campers, put them in canoes, and send them through nearly 150 miles of wilderness. It adds up to a great trip. I know, because I went along.

The expedition, a kind of graduation exercise, marked the close of six summers for boys who attended Camp Kennebec in Maine. The year my turn came we paddled, poled, sailed, and carried our canoes along the Allagash Wilderness Waterway almost to Maine's northernmost tip.

Our adventure starts at a comfortable base camp on the northern end of Chesuncook Lake. We spend nearly a week here while our leaders help us smooth our camping and canoe-poling techniques.

There's a knack to standing up in a canoe and guiding it through swift water with a long pole but we soon get the hang of it. We have plenty of time for paddling practice, too, including a trip to clean up an island left littered by thoughtless fishermen. We vow we'll leave our campsites a whole lot cleaner than those guys left theirs!

The night before we set out, the leaders divide us into two groups. The group I'm with has a dozen other campers and three counselors. We draw lots for paddles, poles, canoes, then load the seaplane that will take our gear to our first night's campsite.

We get an early start— awake at 3:30 in the morning and on the water at 4:30. A motorboat tows us the first six miles across the lake, then we paddle three miles to our first "carry," or "portage." By any name it means haul the canoes out of the water in one place,

pick them up, and carry them to another place. Our first carry is two miles long on a muddy, narrow trail shaded by towering evergreens. In spots we wade in soggy goo almost to our waists and feel very thankful that our camping gear is in the plane and not on our backs.

After the carry we paddle another 15 miles and make camp. The other group goes ahead to a different campsite. We will stay a day apart for the rest of the trip.

For two more days we lake-hop northward. On Churchill Lake we lash our canoes together, rig a tent for a sail, and let the wind push us for an hour and a half. We fall asleep that night talking about the rapids we face the next day, for we are about to enter the Allagash River.

A short paddle takes us to the first rapids, 10 miles of racing water. Our base-camp preparation pays off, for careful work with the poles gets us through with only a couple of canoe swampings and broken poles—a small price for the thrill-packed ride.

Now we feel even more like veteran canoeists, confident we can handle whatever lies ahead. Even a bone-chilling rain does not dampen our spirits. The next day we cover 28 miles, a two-day distance. The long run includes a carry around Allagash Falls and a delay to fish gear out of the river after a canoe capsizes.

Our lunch is in the canoe that turns over. We learn that, despite the un-tarnished look of the wilderness around us, we cannot eat any food touched by river water because of pollution. Only the crackers and cookies stay dry, so they form our lunch menu.

The 28-mile run earns us an extra day's layover. We spend it eating and sleeping. We also clean the gear that will be used by next year's campers, for we're near the end of our river trail. Three hours' paddling the following morning brings us to the bridge at Fort Kent, Maine, our last landmark.

The unforgettable journey has lasted 18 days. The drive back to the town of North Belgrade and Camp Kennebec will take just seven hours.

650 words STOP

Red-Nosed Reindeer

Patricia F. Robbins

Away they fly over the rooftops—Dasher, Dancer, Rudolph, and all the rest. If you think reindeer work hard only one night a year or that a reindeer-powered sleigh is just a myth, you are wrong.

Reindeer are very real indeed, and their "little old driver, so lively and quick" could be a Russian fur trapper who lives in the world's coldest town, Oymyakon, Siberia.

Oymyakon's temperature once plunged to 90°F. below zero. Horses can't stand that kind of deep freeze. Even man's machines find the going rough. But a reindeer feels right at home.

Equipped with long legs, *Rangifer tarandus* digs deep into snowdrifts for his favorite food, a lichen called reindeer moss. Broad hooves serve as both snowshoes and ice skates. A double-layered overcoat protects him from the cold. Inside hairs are dense and oily to keep him dry. Hollow outer hairs trap air, providing both insulation and a buoyant life jacket for icy swims.

Many years ago—no one knows quite when—Lapps began to herd and harness deer. These nomadic people of northern Scandinavia and parts of Russia learned to rely on reindeer for food, clothing, shelter, transportation, and even amusement. Herds provide their owners with milk, meat, and hides for clothing, rugs, and tents. Nothing goes to waste. Hooves boil down into soup stock; sinews sew up Lapp boots; antlers and bones become tools.

Siberians often ride reindeer. Scandinavian Lapps prefer to harness their animals to canoe-shaped sleds called *pulkkas.* Lapp children keep young deer as pets and play at being herders with toy animals carved from bone.

The mid-winter roundup brings *markkina ja juhla,* market and celebration, with reindeer racing as a main event. With a skier or sled skimming behind, each deer speeds around the track. The contestant with the best time wins.

A harnessed reindeer can out-run and outlast a horse—if he has a mind to. Balky as mules, reindeer may bolt or just sit down. Laughter-loving Lapps think it all adds to the fun.

French settlers in Canada called native reindeer by the name caribou [kar′ə-bo͞o′]. They probably borrowed the word from northland Indians. Caribou stand taller than their European relatives and weigh much more. Generations of Indians and Eskimos have hunted caribou, but have never tamed them.

In the late 1800's, smaller, tame reindeer were brought from Europe and Siberia to improve the diet of Eskimos living on the Alaskan coast. These hunters depended on sea mammals for food, but commercial whalers had depleted the supply. A United States official suggested reindeer ranching as a solution and imported Lapp herdsmen to teach the skills.

The reindeer quickly multiplied and spread. A healthy herd doubles its size every three years. Many hoofed immigrants wandered off into the wild with their caribou cousins. Today, *Rangifers* both large and small roam parts of Alaska and Canada.

Reindeer and caribou have something in common that sets them apart from all other deer—females with antlers. Antlers look like handy food-digging tools, but they mostly serve to attract other deer. Sharp hooves do the spadework that nets a hungry reindeer or caribou his daily ration—about 25 pounds of moss.

Both sexes grow new antlers each year, in time for fall mating season. Males soon lose their toppers, but females hold on to their fancy headgear until spring. Since male antlers drop off around Christmastime, the reindeer you see in Yule displays usually are females.

Youngsters probably began linking reindeer with Santa after Clement C. Moore wrote "A Visit from St. Nicholas" nearly 150 years ago. Since then, American children have listened for "the prancing and pawing of each little hoof."

But over in Lapland, children believe the story goes a bit differently. They say the Lapp Santa, *Joulupukki,* borrows all of their pets for his big Christmas ride. Then he returns the reindeer by morning so they can pull their young owners' sleds for another year.

665 words STOP

I thought you would enjoy hearing from a young
friend with some interesting pets.... The Old Observer

Huskies in the Rockies

Bruce Mace

My home is high in Colorado's Rocky Mountains. Each weekday I ride a bus 11 miles to school in Aspen. But on weekends my life goes to the dogs—52 of them. From mid-December to mid-April I help feed, harness, and drive hard-working huskies over the snow. Like the dogs, I'm part of a team—a family team that gives visitors a taste of wilderness adventure.

My father got interested in dog teams during World War II, when he worked with huskies in an Army arctic rescue unit. The experience changed his life. Instead of going back to his job as a botanist, he bought 14 dogs, came here, and built our home, a lodge, restaurant, and kennels near the abandoned mining town of Ashcroft.

I'm the youngest of five children, and we all have helped with the family business. My three brothers and I drove sleds, each one helping teach the next. I began driving with an older brother seven years ago when I was 10. By the time I was 13, I could drive alone.

A dogsled ride feels like nothing else. The motion is something like a hammock's, but forward and back instead of side to side. It makes some people sleepy. Passengers sit bundled up in the sled. The driver rides the runners, shifting his weight to balance the sled and help steer it.

We harness 13 dogs for each team, in pairs attached to a main line that runs from the sled to the lead dog. The lead dog has special training and works alone. He must be a born leader—not necessarily the strongest or the boss, but one willing to take responsibility.

There are no reins. You control the dogs by your voice. We never use a whip.

I carry a rolled-up dog food sack and hit my leg with it to make a sharp noise.

Sled dogs are a lot like mischievous children. They are happy animals, but they sometimes fight. Dogs know if a driver is inexperienced, and they take advantage. They won't work if he yells too much either. A driver has to appreciate his dogs to get the best out of them.

Most of our dogs are a cross between the big, sturdy Alaskan Eskimo dogs called malamutes and smaller, fast Siberian huskies. My father believes mixing the strains makes better working dogs. Each team can easily pull a half-ton load on a good trail.

We give the huskies Eskimo or Indian names, and I know every one of them by name. When I go to pick a team, they all bark and yelp to be chosen that day. I try to mix up the pairs for better spirit. If you change around, the dogs forget yesterday's arguments.

I must also remember where each dog likes to run. They all have favorite spots. Some like the "point," just behind the lead dog. Others prefer the "wheel" position, closest to the sled. Some run best in the middle.

Drivers are called mushers, but we don't start a team off by yelling "mush." Our family says "height," a short version of "all right." We use "gee" and "haw" for right and left; "easy boys" to slow the team; and "whoa" for stop. After you learn the basics, you develop your own special "pepper-uppers," combinations of rhythmic sounds to encourage the dogs. It sounds a little like yodeling.

My father occasionally used our dogs for rescue work until he was injured. Then my brothers and I took over the driving.

Most of our family is grown now, so when I leave for college the kennels probably will close. Older dogs can retire; younger ones will go to other people as pets.

Some people are afraid of huskies because they think the dogs have wolf blood and are vicious. But it just isn't so. Huskies really are very loving animals. After I've said my final good-byes, I know I'll miss them.

STOP

665 words

Trail-Makers
Part 1
Montgomery M. Atwater

Some day you will travel westward, by train, by automobile, or perhaps by airplane. You will cross the Great Plains of the Middle West and on their western edge you will see a great wall rising up, up to the sky, the Rocky Mountains. And as you travel among the deep, winding gorges you may ask yourself as I once did, "How in the world did the men who planned railroad, highway, or air route find their way through such a jumble of canyons and peaks? How did they know which stream, which valley would lead them through?"

You couldn't possibly guess the answer. It was the Trail-Makers who showed the way, the timid deer, the lumbering elk, the lordly moose. Long before men dared set foot in those wild and lonely canyons, the Trail-Makers knew every twist and turn, the source of every stream, the end of every valley. They knew how to reach the lowest passes, those gateways in the mountains, leading to the fertile country on the other side. And their sharp hoofs cut paths through forest, under cliff and over rockslide, paths that men could follow.

First to follow the game trails were the trappers and hunters. These in turn guided settlers and gold seekers who widened the trails into wagon roads. In their footsteps came the railroad builders to lay their ribbons of steel, and the highway engineers to open the way for automobiles. And now the pilot lays his course above highway and railroad as he flies over the mountains with the air mail. Whether they know it or not, they are all following the Trail-Makers.

It is wonderful how skillfully their paths were chosen, taking always the shortest, easiest route. Man with all his surveying instruments, all his notebooks and maps, can hardly improve them. He can only make them wider and smoother. We who live in the wilderness have learned to follow the deer and elk and moose when we are in strange territory.

The deer are the smallest of the Trail-Makers. They grow about as tall as Shetland ponies. But there the resemblance ends. Their bodies are small and their legs so thin and delicate that one wonders how they manage to keep from breaking them. Against their enemies, and they have many, their only protection is speed. How they can run!

It is really incorrect, however, to say that deer run. At full speed they do not gallop; they bound, ten yards and more at a jump, landing with all four feet close together. They go so easily and lightly that it seems as though their muscles must be made of rubber bands.

To warn them of the approach of danger, they have truly marvelous powers of hearing, scent, and sight. Their eyes are like telescopes. Usually they are gone long before an enemy can get close to them. And as they run off they always stick their short tails straight in the air, showing a patch of white fur. From this they get their nickname of White-Tails.

Only the male deer, or bucks, have horns. Each year they lose these horns and grow a new set with a new prong on each antler. In this way a buck always carries with him a record of his age. They are very handsome, those horns, curving gracefully up from their owner's head. And the buck is proud of them. When they are new he will spend hours polishing them against a young pine tree. In the woods one is always coming across small trees with bark in tatters and half the limbs broken off.

605 words

Trail-Makers
Part 2

Montgomery M. Atwater

The elk at first sight resembles his smaller cousin, the deer. He is a good deal the same shape and color. But size is not the only difference. The elk is rather a clumsy animal with none of the speed and grace of the deer. A swift horse can outrun an elk in open country. But what he lacks in speed he makes up in strength. The elk is so big and powerful that he has few enemies in the wilderness.

The horns of a bull elk look a great deal like those of a buck, but are ever so much larger. The Indian name for the elk is "Trees-in-the-Head," and it is a good description. The antlers of an old elk are really immense. Until I found out how they managed it I used to wonder how they ever carried those horns at full speed through thick timber without catching on every tree. This is the answer to the riddle. When he is running, the elk (and the deer too for that matter) throws his head back so that his horns almost touch his sides. In this position all the prongs point to the rear and slide easily among the branches and tree-trunks. Nevertheless, there is always a mighty crackling of dry limbs and scraping of bark when old Trees-in-the-Head goes by.

In the fall the bull elk become quite quarrelsome and have fierce battles with each other, using their horns and front feet as weapons. Many a night I have sat by my campfire and listened to them challenging each other—we call it "bugling"—across the lonely canyons. It is an eerie sound, that long, ringing whistle that seems to come from every direction at once. Except for this one time of year, the elk are the most peaceable folk imaginable.

I cannot say the same for the last and biggest of the Trail-Makers. The moose has a reputation for being quarrelsome at all times of year. Many an innocent camper has spent part of a night in a tree simply because he disturbed his lordship. Perhaps he acts this way because he is the real monarch of the wilderness and wants to make sure that everyone knows it.

A full-grown moose is a tremendous animal, taller than a horse, almost black in color, with great, long legs and wide-spreading horns. It is from his antlers that the moose gets his nickname, Shovel-Horns. They are broad and wide, just like shovels with a row of spikes around the rim. Hanging down from his throat, Shovel-Horns has a tassel of fur about six inches long, called the "bell."

These three are the Trail-Makers of the mountains. I only wish there were space to tell you something about the Trail-Makers of the plains. Surely you have heard of the buffalo, that shaggy character who has a part in every pioneer story. He helped men on the road westward by leading them to water holes. And then there was the antelope whose tiny feet once cut paths where now broad highways go toward the setting sun.

The caribou is Trail-Maker of the North. Even today men are following his footprints farther and farther into the unknown wildernesses near the Arctic Circle. Each fall these strange animals gather into herds of hundreds and thousands and move southward for the winter. This is called the caribou migration. Nothing can turn it aside. Across deep rivers, over high mountains, through swamps and forests the great mass pushes on.

But after all I think that the deer, elk, and moose have helped men most. Had it not been for them the mountains might have barred the way for a hundred years. So when your train or your automobile climbs smoothly up the narrow gorges to the pass, or your airplane swings high above the peaks and canyons, think of White-Tail and Trees-in-the-Head and Shovel-Horns who led the way.

665 words STOP

A Bridge of Monkeys

Author Unknown

For many days we had been pushing our way through one of the densest forests of South America. Late one afternoon, we stopped by the side of a swift, narrow river and began to set up camp for the night. Suddenly we heard a loud chattering and screaming coming from the other side of the stream. It sounded as if thousands of monkeys were moving through the trees toward us, each trying to make more noise than all the rest.

"It's an army of monkeys on the march," said our guide. "They're coming this way and will most likely cross the river over there." He pointed to a place where the steep banks were clothed with tall trees on either side.

"How will they cross there?" I asked, amazed. "The water is so swift that they certainly can't swim across."

"Oh, no," said the guide; "monkeys would rather go through fire than water. If they can't leap the stream, they will bridge it."

"Bridge it! And how will they do that?"

"Wait a bit, and you'll see," replied the guide.

We could now plainly see the animals making their way through the treetops and approaching the place the guide had pointed out. In front was an old gray-headed monkey who directed all their movements and seemed to be the general-in-chief of the army. Here and there were other officers, each appearing to have certain duties to perform.

One of the officers ran out along an overhanging branch and, after looking across the stream as if to measure the distance, scampered back to make a report to the leader. There was at once a change in the conduct of the army. Commands were given, and a number of able-bodied monkeys were marched to the front. Then several ran along the bank, examining the trees on both sides.

After a time, all gathered near a tall cottonwood tree that grew over the narrowest part of the stream, and twenty or thirty of them climbed its trunk. The foremost—a strong fellow—ran out on a limb and, winding his tail around it, slipped off, head hanging downward. The next on the limb climbed down the body of the first and, wrapping his tail tightly around him, dropped off in his turn and hung head downward. In the same manner the third monkey fastened himself to the second, and the fourth to the third, and so on, until the last one on the string rested his forepaws on the ground.

The living chain now commenced swinging backward and forward like a pendulum. The motion was slight at first but gradually increased, the monkey at the lower end striking his hands against the ground and pushing out with all his strength. This was kept up until the bottom monkey was able to grab one of the branches on the opposite bank. The chain now reached from one side of the stream to the other, forming a living bridge over which all the other monkeys, young and old, passed without confusion or delay.

The army was soon safely across, but how were the animals forming the bridge to get themselves over? If the monkey at the top of the chain were to let go of his branch, the other end of the bridge was so much lower that he and all those nearest him would be dashed against the opposite bank or plunged into the water.

The question was soon answered. A powerful fellow on the other side took firm hold of the lowest monkey on the bridge; then another fastened himself to him in like manner, and this was continued until a dozen or more were added to the string. These last monkeys then ran up to a high limb and lifted that end of the bridge until it was several feet above the end on the opposite bank.

Then the monkey who had formed the first link of the chain unwound his tail from the cottonwood branch, and the whole bridge swung safely over. The lowermost links dropped lightly to the ground, while the higher ones leaped to the branches. The whole army then scampered away into the forest, and the sound of their chattering was soon lost in the distance.

710 words **STOP**

Storm Warnings

Severe storms can cause catastrophic damage. Heavy rains and flash floods, thunder, and lightning can happen anywhere . . . and often with little or no warning. You can't stop them, and you can't outrun them. But you can outsmart them.

Flash floods usually happen when heavy rains come over a very short period of time, after widespread melting of snow, or after a dam breaks.

Flash floods tend to come on very suddenly. Their racing waters are so powerful that a 6-inch-deep stream can knock down a person. Deeper floodwaters can sweep cars and buses off roads, wash out bridges, and lift houses right off their foundation.

To be safe in a flash flood, you've got to get above it. If you are in a car, climb on top of it to get out of the oncoming flood's pathway. If you are in a stream bed or valley, drop everything you're carrying and scramble up on top of rocks, climb up the hillside, or climb a tree.

In the city, racing gutter water acts just like flash flood water. Stay clear of street drains, and don't try to wade through the water that is racing toward the drains.

Lightning bolts can split tree trunks, start fires, and knock out phone and power lines. They can burn down buildings and homes, burst water pipes, burn out electrical wiring, and fry electrical appliances and equipment. They can injure or kill people and animals.

The state with the greatest number of lightning strikes is Florida. That's because lightning loves heat and humidity, and Florida has lots of both. The second highest number of lightning strikes occur in midwestern states. That's because those states have many tornadoes, and tornadoes produce lightning.

Where there's thunder, there is lightning. If you can hear thunder, there is lightning, too, even if you can't see it. This is true of severe thunderstorms, with their super dark clouds and sudden wind shifts that occur from early May through early September.

Here are some weather-wise tips for staying safe when a storm is brewing and lightning strikes.

- Do not leave the house or building you are in.
- Close all windows and outside doors. Pull down blinds or shades.

Lightning can produce "side-flashes," which can enter a home through an open window.

- Stay off the phone. Lightning can travel through the phone line to you.
- Unplug all electrical equipment and appliances, including the phone. To listen to weather reports, use a battery-powered radio.
- Do not run water. Water pipes often carry lightning into the house.
- Stay away from metal appliances, bathroom fixtures, and electrical fuse boxes. All conduct electricity.
- Move to the side of the building that faces away from the oncoming storm.
- If you are outside, go inside a building.
- If no buildings are around, get into a car and roll up the windows.
- If you are swimming or boating, get out of the water immediately and get as far away from the water as possible. Water does not just conduct electricity, it attracts it.
- If a lightning storm catches you without shelter, head for the lowest area around— the base of a hill, a waterless ditch, a dip between two hills. Squat or crouch with knees drawn up and both feet together. Do not let your hands touch the ground. Never lie flat on the ground. Your fully ex-

tended body gives lightning a bigger target.

- *Don't* take cover under a tree. Many lightning fatalities happen when trees are struck.
- If you are in a group, spread out.
- If you are near metal—wire fencing, sports equipment, a bicycle—get as far away from it as possible. If you are carrying or using metal articles—a backpack, pocket knife, umbrella, house keys, golf clubs—throw them as far away as possible.
- If water begins to accumulate around you and you are in a low-lying area, move to higher ground.

Between 250 and 350 Americans are struck by lightning every year. Most of them survive with few injuries. Some, however, need immediate medical attention. If you are with a person who has been struck, cover him or her with a jacket or blanket to keep the person warm, and then get to the nearest phone and call 911.

Storms are part of nature—and we haven't seen the last of them, that's for certain. But you can stay safe from the dangers they may inflict by brushing up on your safety sense—before the next storm warnings rumble in.

750 words STOP

Who Goes There?

"Who, who-o, who-o-o, who-o-o." Who has the biggest ears of any bird? Meet the great horned owl. Hooty needs big ears. "The better to hear you, my dear," he says about a fat rat running across the dry leaves on the forest floor. The great horned owl has super hearing! His big ears on the side of his head cannot be seen, because they are covered by pretty brown and white feathers. But how do soft sounds from a mouse that is scurrying through the woods get through those feathers and into Hooty's ears?

The wise old owl's *eyes* give us the answer! Have you noticed how they are sunken in his head? The great Creator built them that way for a reason. The feathers around each eye are formed in the shape of a saucer. Those little "saucers" trap exciting sounds and send them through special channels under his feathers to his ears. If the owl didn't have those feathers around his eyes to collect sounds, he would starve to death, because Hooty finds most of his food through sounds, and after dark!

High on a pine tree limb after sundown, the great horned owl turns his head toward the ground. Slowly, he moves it back and forth until his very sensitive ears hear a rustling in the leaves below. He moves his head back a little until the sound comes in loudest. You see, the saucer-shaped feathers around his eyes make his hearing very directional. The big bird silently soars down, keeping his ears tuned to the sound. Suddenly, he turns his head a little to zero in better on the sound. No wonder he can find a little mouse after dark!

Of course, his good eyes help greatly, too! Scientists say the great horned owl's eyes are one hundred times more sensitive to faint light than human eyes. He can control his pupils. Hooty opens his pupils wide after dark. The light from the stars is just perfect for wise old owl, and he lets all the available light in. Think for a moment how much you can see on a moonlit night! Then multiply this one hundred times for Hooty. He may even have to make his pupils smaller to let in less light. Quite a clever hunter, isn't he?

Do you know the owl's favorite meal? Well hang onto your nose, because it's fresh skunk. *Mm!* The great horned owl doesn't give a hoot about the smell. While br'er skunk is turning over rocks looking for grubs and beetles, Hooty sails in silently, sinks his terribly sharp claws into the skunk and—that's all! Fresh skunk is on the table.

But why didn't the skunk get out of the way? Couldn't he hear the owl swooping in? That's just the trouble—he couldn't! Hooty sailed in on *silent* wings. His wings don't make noise like those of most birds. When the Lord Jesus Christ, the Creator, designed the great horned owl's wings, He made very special feathers, not like those of other birds. The wing feathers of an owl have soft, downy edges. Those downy feathers muffle any wing sounds, and the big bird flies in perfect silence through the woods at night. No wonder he's able to catch his food. Do you see evidence of a Creator in Mr. Owl?

All night long the big hunter swoops down on small animals. Most of the time he gets mice who are nibbling at the farmer's crops. With one bite, Hooty swallows one of the little rodents whole: fur, bones, teeth, tail, and all! But does the owl digest *all* of that? Of course not! It would kill him if he tried. The mouse's sharp teeth and bones would puncture Hooty's stomach. But here is where the intelligent Creator really did a marvelous job! He gave the owl a special stomach acid that eats away at the fur and bones and leaves only the meat for the big bird to digest.

How does Hooty get rid of the fur, teeth, and bones? God gave him a very special compartment at the top of his stomach that picks up the bones and fur, and a muscle that slowly pushes them up the owl's throat. Won't this hurt his esophagus? Not at all! He has many gastric cell glands in his throat that manufacture thick, slippery mucus. This mucus coats the bones and fur so they will slip up his esophagus safely as the muscle pushes. Then, *errpp:* Hooty's sharp bill opens and a three-inch-long pellet falls out and tumbles to the ground. A wonderful design, isn't it?

The old fellow settles down on a limb high in the big oak tree and goes to sleep. It's morning, and our night hunter is tired and wants to go to bed. His claws lock around the limb, holding him safely in place for a nice day's nap.

820 words STOP

I Spy on Wild Animals from a Treetop Hotel

George Crossette

Almost every child dreams of building a tree house. But few have ever imagined a hideaway as glorious as Treetops, a "hotel in the trees" built by Eric Sherbrooke Walker.

Just as you admit only friends to your tree-house club, so Mr. Walker's guests are those who, like him, admire East Africa's fabulous wildlife.

He and his visitors are lords of all they survey from the windows and balconies of Treetops. Elephants, rhinos, hyenas, buffaloes, and many other animals graze and water below as freely as though no human existed within miles. Elephants often scratch themselves on the thick posts supporting the lodge. Their bumping and rubbing give the effect of a minor earthquake.

Kenya's most famous water hole attracts the roving beasts, and the world's most unusual hotel lures nature lovers to this wooded spot 100 miles north of Nairobi.

When you visit Tree-tops, your Land-Rover stops short, and you walk the last quarter mile through the Aberdare forest, staying close to a guide with a powerful rifle. You climb into the lodge by stairs drawn up after you.

In the parlor, you sign the guest book and are shown to your room. In the hallways you duck under tree limbs and step over branches which shoot through the building like a web of exposed rafters.

I arrived about three o'clock and climbed quickly to the observation roof. Within half an hour animals began to appear, the small ones first. By four, I had counted over 100 creatures, including buffaloes, hyenas, bush pigs, the rare giant forest hogs, bushbucks, waterbucks, monkeys, and baboons.

Two lady baboons are invited to tea each afternoon at 4:30. They bring their clinging babies and are quite accustomed to the constant clicking of the camera.

As the afternoon progresses, more animals appear. One can hardly believe so many different types could be attracted to an area so small. Attendants turn on floodlights so the animals will not be frightened by sudden artificial light after dark.

You will find it difficult to take time out for dinner, for that is when the larger animals begin to gather. Some observers never leave their balcony chairs during the entire night.

At eight o'clock we counted 58 elephants, 26 rhinos, and some 200 buffaloes, all milling around the pool's edge—drinking and searching for the much-prized salt put out as bait. The elephants use their feet to press pockets into the muddy ground near the pond. As the water seeps in, they drink to their heart's content. When these huge beasts are satisfied, the smaller animals take advantage of their work and rush in to drink from the holes.

Elephants and rhinos fight for favorite spots. Occasionally one charges the other, the result usually a draw. There is a definite "pecking order." Elephants drink whenever they wish, followed by the rhinos. Next come the giant hogs, their eyes shining like red beads in the floodlights. Then the bushbucks take their turn.

Treetops opened in 1932. Since then, many thousands of people, no more than 40 at a time, have enjoyed this bird's-eye view of African wildlife. The structure was enlarged in 1957 after the Mau Mau burned the old one. At the original Treetops, in 1952, England's Elizabeth climbed the stairs a princess and came down a queen, for it was there that she learned of the death of her father, King George VI.

Eric Walker enjoys answering the questions of guests. Most of them concern the elephant. While a herd tramples below, you learn that elephants sometimes reach 150 years of age and weigh seven to 12 tons. Each one eats approximately 800 pounds of fodder a day. His tusks weigh as much as 150 pounds each. The elephant is one of the few animals known to help a sick or wounded comrade. There are many recorded instances where two members of the herd supported a wounded companion for some distance.

Second in popularity is the rhinoceros. These monstrous beasts are surprisingly light on their feet. They appear to dance as they run and turn quickly. Like a polo pony, they can turn within their own length while at a full run. Yet they are extremely noisy on occasion and can be heard fighting a mile away.

Rhinos have mouths so tough they can eat dried, leafless branches with enormous thorns without apparent discomfort.

The buffalo, considered by many to be Africa's most dangerous game, is the third most popular animal visitor. He is feared because he frequently turns the tables on man. While man hunts him, he in turn hunts man for sport, frequently circling in an attempt to come up behind the hunter. Because of his cunning he is responsible for many human deaths.

I could not overlook the abundant birdlife at Treetops. White egrets sit unmolested on the backs of the grazing African buffaloes. Entire duck families scoot around the lily pads or walk along the water's edge.

Hornbills and vultures hover overhead while storks—flying directly from chimney nests in Amsterdam—wade in the shallow water. One ornithologist has listed more than 90 different bird species at the hotel.

Treetops weaves such a spell that few guests leave willingly. I lingered as long as I dared, thinking of all I could see and do if I had just one more day.

STOP

900 words

72

The Oyster Thief

It's fun to go to the ocean and see what the tide has brought in. Pieces of driftwood, seaweed, and pretty shells dot the soft sand. Here and there we find a broken seashell, a piece of coral, a couple of sand dollars, a conch, and—what's this? It's a starfish. Sure it's dead, or it wouldn't be lying in the sand. Oh, it's so beautiful! It has five perfectly shaped arms. It looks exactly like a star. It's not soft, as you'd expect a fish to be, but instead its dried-out body is prickly. Thousands of tiny, sharp spines cover it from the tip of one arm to the tip of the others. In fact, that is why the starfish belongs to a group of sea creatures called *echinoderms*. *Echinoderm* means "spiny skin." The ancient Greeks made up the word. *Echino* means "spiny," and *derm* means "skin."

Our starfish treasure is yellowish orange and is about five inches across. Some starfish grow as large as three feet across. The smallest ones grow to be only one-half inch across.

Christ, the Creator, made starfish in several different colors. Red, pink, orange, and yellow are the most common starfish colors. However, some starfish are purple, green, blue, or gray.

The Master Designer didn't make all starfish with five arms. He likes variety, so the Lord made some to have only three arms, others six or seven, some twenty, and a few with up to fifty arms. Marine biologists have figured that there are at least two thousand different species of starfish. Some were meant to live in deep ocean water, whereas others live in shallow water. Every ocean of the world has starfish. After starfish have spent about five adventurous years on the sandy bottom, they die, and the currents and tides carry their bodies onto the shore, where they dry in the warm sunshine.

What is the starfish like in the ocean? Scientists have learned much about this amazing and beautiful sea creature. It's so complicated and fantastically engineered that you would declare it must have been built under a powerful microscope.

The thousands of tiny, sharp spines on the top of the starfish's arms and central body are very important. Without them he couldn't protect himself from little sea animals that want to attach themselves to his body and rob him of strength. If you looked at those spines under a microscope, they would look like tiny jaws that open and close. When some tiny sea creature or algae wants to attach itself to the starfish, the sensitive cells in the starfish's skin tell his spiney "jaws" to "bite" the animal. That naturally keeps the tiny invaders away and protects the starfish from becoming covered with parasites.

Think of it. There are thousands of protective spines on each arm, and that's a lot if the starfish has fifty arms. Furthermore, each little "jaw" can be operated by itself. How could something so complicated have ever gotten here through the chancy process of evolution? Doesn't the starfish show evidence of intelligence and planning? Where did intelligence come from?

A starfish's body looks like a bicycle wheel. The center disk, the hub, is attached to five arms, or spokes.

The starfish's mouth is on the *bottom* side of his body in the center of the hub. From the mouth there is a groove running out to the end of each arm. Those grooves are really a super job of engineering by Christ, the Creator. In each groove there are two to four rows of very small feet. They are called *tube feet*. Each tube foot has a tiny suction cup at its tip. With those suction cups the starfish walks, traveling about three inches per minute.

At the end of each arm, or tentacle, the starfish has many cells that are very sensitive to light. They're sort of like eyes.

As the starfish travels slowly through the water, his special cells and sensitive tube feet tell him that he has walked right into the middle of a bed of yummy oysters. *Mm!* Starfish love to eat oysters.

When the oysters discover that the starfish has arrived, they tuck in their soft bodies and close their shells—*snap!* But that doesn't help them any. The starfish climbs over the oyster shell and feels where the shell should open. With one arm on one side of the shell and another tentacle on the other side, the starfish turns on the pumps in his arms, causing the suction cups in each tube foot to grab firmly onto the shell. With his strong arms he tries to pull the shell open. But the oyster has a strong muscle in the hinge of his shell.

Finally, the oyster tires a little and lets his shell open about as wide as a piece of cardboard is thick. The starfish knows that and does something very strange. With a muscle he pulls his stomach out of his mouth! His stomach is about as thick as a piece of cardboard, so the starfish slips his stomach, *inside out,* into the thin crack of the oyster's shell. The starfish then manufactures powerful digestive juice and squirts it on the oyster's body. That numbs the oyster and breaks down the solid part of his body so that the starfish can digest him. The starfish actually eats the oyster while it is still in its "closed" shell.

When the starfish is finished dining, he pulls his stomach out of the shell and goes his merry way. Some great design, isn't it? Think for a while about what a fantastic, superintelligent creator the Lord Jesus Christ is.

920 words STOP

76

The Trap-Door Spider

It's evening in Australia, and a centipede scrambles over the ground, nervously searching for food. Suddenly a hole appears in the earth, and a big, brown spider jumps out and grabs the centipede. Quick as a flash the spider drags the paralyzed myriapod to his den and the hole disappears.

Were our eyes playing tricks on us? No, they weren't. What we "saw" was an amazing underground engineer at work,

the Australian trap-door spider. Let's call him T.D. for short.

T.D. is brown and about an inch long. He lives in a very comfortable home that has silk, wall-to-wall carpeting, spun by the spider himself. His home is waterproof and insectproof. He has a specially engineered lid on his den that gives him his name, trap-door spider. He pushes the lid up with his head and peeks out, looking for food. You'd never know the trapdoor was there. It's the color of the ground around it, camouflaged beautifully with little pieces of moss. But when it swings open suddenly, *beware Mr. Bug!* Here comes the trap-door spider!

T.D. doesn't build his home just *anywhere.* He chooses a high spot where rainwater won't form into puddles. Old "eight-legs" doesn't want to open his trapdoor and get a surprise bath, even though he can swim.

After T.D. has selected the perfect spot for his home, he bites the ground. His mouth is amazing. It's a fantastic shovel with a row of teeth on the bottom jaw and two fangs. With those tools, T.D. digs into the earth and comes up with a mouthful of little stones and dirt. He walks over to his dirt pile nearby and unloads, going back and forth between hole and pile again and again until he has a hole one foot deep and one and one-half inches wide. The hole looks like a laboratory test tube.

Next T.D. orders the carpet for his den. He wants the floor, walls, and ceiling covered with silk, one-eighth of an inch thick. In T.D.'s body, Christ the Creator put several liquid silk glands. Spiders use those "factories" to make their sticky webs. The trap-door spider's brain sends an electrical signal to a muscle in his abdomen that squeezes out several fine strands of sticky, liquid silk through openings called spinnerets. With his hind legs, T.D. twists those strands of liquid silk into one strong strand, just the way you would make a rope. When air strikes the silk strand, it dries and becomes strong and elasticlike. Time and again the spider does this, until he has covered every inch of his dirt house with silk. The silk carpet keeps T.D. warm and dry. Also, other insects can't burrow through the tough, sticky carpet.

Now work begins on the trapdoor. First T.D. scampers around, looking for a piece of sun-baked mud. When he finds a chunk about two inches wide, he drags it over to his den. With his teeth and fangs he cuts it in the shape of a circle, a little bigger than the opening of his house. T.D. doesn't use a tape measure as we do. His four precision eyes tell him exactly how large to make the lid. He's intelligent! The spider chips away at the piece of sun-baked mud until it's only one-fourth of an inch thick. Then T.D. cuts a little

bevel on the edge of his lid. Soon he'll do the same to the top of his hole. Those beveled surfaces will match each other perfectly so that his door will fit snugly.

The trapdoor is finished. Now T.D. must waterproof it. So he spins more strands of sticky liquid silk, covering the top, bottom, and sides of his trapdoor. The air quickly hardens the silk. Next our eight-legged engineer drags his door to where just a little of it hangs over the edge of the den. T.D. crawls down inside about half an inch, holding onto his silk carpet wall. Then he grabs the edge of his trapdoor and pulls it over the hole. "Ah, just the right size," T.D. says to himself with a chuckle.

"Now I'd better put the hinge on," T.D. says. But before T.D. can put the hinge on, he has to make it. And what do you think he makes it out of? That's right, silk! So down in his dark hole the trap-door spider spins a silk hinge, attaching one end of the tough strand to the underside edge of the lid and the other end to the top of his silk wall. T.D. adds more and more strands to the little hinge until he knows there are enough.

Next T.D. tests his door. With his feet and head he lifts the trapdoor, and it swings open ninety degrees. Then he backs down into his hole, with one of his clawlike feet grabs a little silk handle he made under the lid, and pulls the trapdoor shut. Sometimes when the ornery hunting wasp tries to get into T.D.'s den, T.D. has to hold the door shut. It's good he made the handle strong.

Finally the trap-door spider puts the finishing touches on his house. He pushes the door open with his head and crawls out. He comes back with tiny pieces of moss to camouflage his trapdoor. With liquid silk he sticks them to the lid. Really a beautiful cover-up!

His house is finished. T.D. crawls down into his den, waiting for that centipede. With the lid propped open just enough to see out, T.D. waits for the little myriapod. There he is! He just ran over the top of T.D.'s house. Quick as a flash the trapdoor swings open and T.D. grabs the wiggling insect with his fangs. The struggle is soon over. T.D. backs into his den with the centipede in his mouth, reaches up with one foot, and pulls the trapdoor down. Dinner is served.

985 words

80

Lewis and Clark Open the Door to the West

Charles H. Sloan

As the world marched into the 1800s, most of North America flew foreign flags. England pushed to the Pacific; Russia claimed Alaska; and Spain threatened to block the Mississippi. President Thomas Jefferson knew the frontiersmen of the young United States would go to war to keep their river artery open, and war he did not want. So when France agreed to sell the sprawling Louisiana Territory, which it had secretly acquired from Spain, Jefferson was ready. Years later, the purchase would become six states and part of 11 others—all for two and a half cents an acre! The next

*step was the Pacific, and
again Jefferson was pre-
pared. He launched the
Lewis and Clark Expedition
with this order: "Explore
the Missouri river, and such
principal streams of it,
as . . . may offer the most di-
rect communication across
this continent."*

"More mud than water,"
Missouri River veterans describe it.

The tan-colored flood
seems to slide instead of
flow toward the Mississippi.
Sawyers—logs with one end
anchored and the other bobbing above the surface—jab
like lances at human tres-
passers.

Churning water under-
cuts soft banks and drops
them into the current with
enough force to swamp a
boat. Sandbars appear,
shift from shore to shore,
become dry islands then
sink overnight.

But for Meriwether
Lewis and William Clark,
the Missouri River is a
highway to the Rockies.
Across the mountains, an-
other great river, the Columbia, speeds them to the
Pacific Ocean.

Along the way, they
meet Indians with terms of
trade instead of conquest,
pass scenery beyond the
imagination of geographers,
and see animals, birds, and
plants unheard of in the
East.

The adventure begins
beside still another river,
the Potomac. In Washing-
ton, D.C., President Thomas
Jefferson asks his private
secretary, Meriwether
Lewis, to lead the expedition and choose a co-
captain. Jefferson and
Lewis have dreamed of such
an expedition for years.
Now Lewis invites William
Clark to help command it.

On May 21, 1804, the brave band leaves St. Charles, the last town it will see for more than two years.

For five months they push up the treacherous Missouri. Clark usually commands the boats; Lewis explores the shore. Their 55-foot keel-boat and two slim rowing boats average only 10 miles a day.

Near the center of what is now North Dakota, the men build Fort Mandan, named for nearby Indians, to wait out the winter months. A French trapper joins them to serve as interpreter. His Indian wife, Sacagawea, is to become an important part of the expedition.

In April, 1805, the 31 men, Sacagawea, and her baby son set out.

Notebooks get fuller every day. Lewis jots down comments on grizzly bears: ". . . by no means as . . . dan-gerous as they have been represented." Later he admits, "I must confess that I do not like the gentlemen and had rather fight two Indians than one bear."

One day, the group finds two rivers flowing together. The men say the north fork, which Lewis christens the Marias, leads to the Missouri's source. But the two captains have developed a knack for reading the land: The expedition turns up the south fork.

A few days later, at the Great Falls of the Missouri, they know they have guessed well. Indians have told them the Missouri bursts from the Rockies in a series of falls.

Clark marks an 18-mile portage around the cascading water. It takes the men a month to push, pull, and carry their gear to the other end.

Sacagawea becomes their guide. She lived in this region until raiding Indians carried her away when she was about 12 years old.

At Three Forks, where the Jefferson, Madison, and Gallatin Rivers meet to form the Missouri, the Shoshoni squaw shows Lewis and Clark where she was captured.

Again the two captains have to use their knack for geography. The Jefferson and Madison are nearly the same size. Which leads farthest into the mountains? Again they guess well. They choose the Jefferson.

The way gets harder. Soon the expedition must move overland, and for this the men need horses. And to get horses, they must meet the Shoshoni.

Lewis hikes ahead with three men. On August 12, 1805, they become the first white Americans to stand on the Continental Divide. In the valley beyond, they finally find Indians.

Lewis drops his rifle as a sign of peace. The Shoshoni chief throws his arms over the explorer's shoulders. Other Indians do the same until all the white men are "all carressed and besmeared with their grease and paint till . . . heartily tired of the national hug."

After the hugging, the explorers swap trinkets for 29 horses.

They believe they will cross the mountains quickly and find a swift stream to the Pacific. But it is October 7 before the brave band cruises the Snake River. They see more Indians on the way, and again Sacagawea is a help—a woman with a party of men is a sign of peace.

As the explorers speed down the Snake and into the Columbia, the Indians become less agreeable and drive harder bargains. White men cruising the coast have made them wise to the ways of trade.

In November, the group rides the rolling swells of the Columbia estuary through wind and driving rain. Suddenly the skies clear. Ahead the river straightens and widens into a great bay.

"Ocian in view! O! the joy," writes Clark in his journal. They have reached the Pacific.

The weary men built Fort Clatsop near today's Oregon, and settle down until spring, when they return eastward.

Near modern-day Missoula, Montana, they split to explore different paths. On the Marias River, Lewis narrowly escapes death in the expedition's only Indian fight; near the Yellowstone, Crow tribesmen steal some of Clark's horses.

In August, 1806, the groups meet on the Missouri. St. Louis is only a few weeks away. They reach it on September 23.

The grimy, bearded men in Indian garb have opened the West for the United States.

1,015 words STOP

Grenfell of Labrador

Donna Covey

Wilfred Grenfell (1865–1940) was used to adventure. As a boy, he and his brother often traveled into the swamps and countryside near their home in England searching for animals to study. Sometimes they would go out on fishing boats for several days. Though young Wilfred was not aware of it, these early adventures were part of God's preparation for service.

While he was at college studying medicine, Wilfred Grenfell realized that something was missing in his life. One evening he attended an evangelistic meeting, and through the preaching of the famous American revivalist Dwight L. Moody and the testimony of the English missionary C. T. Studd, Wilfred Grenfell accepted Christ as his Savior.

Soon he began teaching a Sunday school class and

holding meetings in a poor section of London. After medical school, he became a missionary doctor among the fishermen of Europe's North Sea. He did his work from a hospital boat. As he took care of the fishermen's wounds, he told them of Christ. Because the mission board that had sent him to the North Sea realized his exceptional love of nature and his bravery in the face of danger, they decided to send him to a place across the sea that needed a doctor and a missionary. This place was the cold wilderness of Labrador, the tundra area of Canada's northeastern coast. He was originally put there to help the fishermen from France and England who had settled in this difficult region, but soon he was working with the Inuits and Indians as well.

To let people know he was there, Dr. Grenfell visited by snow sled from igloo to igloo. In one hand was his medicine bag; in the other was a Bible. Dr. Grenfell was always available when a need arose. He traveled hours over the snow to take care of the sick; in his first three months he treated nine hundred patients. Because the people needed a hospital, he found businessmen in St. John's, Newfoundland, who would pay for one, and he brought in doctors and nurses from England and the United States to help with the medical work. To provide needed supplies, he established a chain of trading posts. Because the people needed more food and work, he gave them jobs at the hospitals, nursing stations, and trading posts. He brought three hundred reindeer from Lapland (northern Norway, Sweden, and Finland) along with Lapp men to teach the people of Labrador how to care for them. He taught the people how to raise plants under glass so that they would already be growing by the time the snow had melted and could be planted outside.

Once Dr. Grenfell found an injured boy who had been left on the shore to die. He nursed him to health, and when he found that he had no place to go, he started an orphanage and a school.

Many ships were damaged at sea, causing loss of life and supplies. To meet this need, Grenfell built a dry dock for repairing ships. He knew that God has promised to supply our needs, and he taught this to the people of Labrador in a

way they could never forget. Many trusted Christ through his testimony.

One of Dr. Grenfell's adventures almost ended in tragedy. As he was walking home from church on an Easter Sunday, a boy ran to him from the hospital to say that a dog team had traveled sixty miles from a village on the other side of the Hudson Bay to get a doctor for a boy who was in critical condition. Wilfred Grenfell quickly prepared his own faithful team of dogs—Brin, Doc, Spy, Moody, Watch, Jerry, and Jack—for the emergency trip.

Because it was springtime, he knew there was great danger of the sled breaking through the slowly melting ice that covered Hudson Bay, but the boy must be saved. Quickly, the supplies were loaded, the team was hitched, and

Grenfell was on his way across the ice. By nightfall, he reached a small village, where he fed the dogs and gathered the people for prayer before he slept.

The wind changed during the night, bringing fog and rain. The next morning's drive of forty miles would be extremely perilous, and there was not a single village along the way. High waves of the night before had broken up the ice on the bay, so that there were huge chasms between one ice pan and the next. He found a long bridge of ice that looked safe, however, and he skillfully maneuvered the team over it.

Suddenly, the ice broke, and Grenfell and his dogs were in the icy water. They managed to scramble to a tiny ice "raft," where they sat exhausted to wait for the end. But no, he could not give up yet. There was a boy's life still to be saved, and many others after that. Using all his wits, and with the help of his faithful dogs, Grenfell managed to get to a larger ice pan, where he could do nothing but pray for a miracle. For warmth, he killed his smaller dogs one by one and wrapped their fur around him. For comfort from hunger, he chewed for twenty-four hours on a rubber band he had been using to hold up his sock.

Then the miracle began to happen. The wind, which had been driving him out to sea, fell. The current began carrying him toward a little village by the sea. Hour after hour, he stood on the ice pan waving his shirt to attract attention. Finally, off in the distance, he saw the hull of a boat that was making its way toward him through the ice-filled water. He was saved! How had his rescuers found him? As he questioned them, miracle after miracle of unusual circumstances unfolded. He has recorded them all in his true adventure book, *Adrift on an Ice Pan.*

Before long, Grenfell, dried out, warmed, and fed by the thankful villagers, started out with a larger team to race back to the hospital, where he had been reported missing. A few days later, the boy who had been so ill was brought to the hospital on a boat, and his life was saved.

At the age of seventy, after forty years of selfless service, a heart attack caused Wilfred Grenfell to retire from Labrador, but not from God's work. He spoke throughout the United States, encouraging others to help the people of the far north. He also wrote several books, including *Adrift on an Ice Pan, The Romance of Labrador,* and *Vikings of Today.* He left behind him in Labrador six hospitals, four hospital ships, seven nursing stations, two orphanages, two large schools, fourteen industrial centers, and a lumber mill. In appreciation for his great work, the English government made him a knight, and he is still known to people around the world as "Grenfell of Labrador."

STOP

1,160 words

Reading Record
and
Quizzes

Reading Record

Selection	Words/Minute	Grade
Pilgrims, Indians, and Thanksgiving		
Hippos at Home		
The Incredible Ear		
Nature's Sandpiles		
Raindrop Miracles		
Mollusk Mansions		
Up and Away in a Hot-Air Balloon		
Summer Ice Storms		
The Pincushion		
Beaver Business		
The Valiant Horse		
Michigan's Magic Island		
The Windmill: Energy's Friend		
The Unchanging Bible and Science		
The Blossoming Tulip Business		
Homing Pigeon Heroes		
The Real Scoop about Ice Cream		
Squid Tricks		
Riding the Rapids		
Red-Nosed Reindeer		

Selection	Words/Minute	Grade
Huskies in the Rockies		
Trail-Makers, Part 1		
Trail-Makers, Part 2		
A Bridge of Monkeys		
Storm Warnings		
Who Goes There?		
I Spy on Wild Animals from a Treetop Hotel		
The Oyster Thief		
The Trap-Door Spider		
Lewis and Clark Open the Door to the West		
Grenfell of Labrador		

Directions: *Circle the correct answer.*

1. How many settlers got off the *Mayflower* in December 1620?

      a. 109   **c.** 99

      b. 90   **d.** 190

2. True or False: Samoset greeted the Pilgrims in English.

3. What had happened to Squanto's entire clan?

      a. They had been massacred.

      b. They had been sent to England.

      c. They had died of a disease.

      d. They had been sold as slaves.

4. True or False: Squanto had once been a slave in Spain.

5. Which Pilgrim governor declared the first Thanksgiving?

      a. John Carver   **b.** William Bradford   **c.** Miles Standish

6. What helped Plimoth Plantation to prosper?

      a. The settlers were healthy and strong.

      b. The Indians and Pilgrims worked together.

      c. England sent money and supplies.

Name _____

Directions: *Circle or write the correct answer.*

_____ %

_____ wpm

1. The Greeks named this huge animal
   hippopotamus because its head somewhat
   resembles the head of a

   _____.

2. When do hippos usually eat?
   a. in the morning
   b. at night
   c. during the hottest part of the day

3. Which are the world's largest land creatures?
   a. elephants   **b.** hippos   **c.** rhinoceroses

4. True or False: Hippos can keep their bodies underwater and still
   see and breathe above the water.

5. Baby hippos are born ___?___ .
   a. on the riverbank   **c.** in grassy fields
   b. underwater   **d.** under shady trees

6. On what continent do hippopotamuses live?
   a. Asia   **c.** South America
   b. Africa   **d.** Australia

7. Which probably hurts the hippo the most?
   a. a spear   **b.** the sun   **c.** its enemies

Bonus: True or False: Hippos eat fish and small land animals.

Number of words: 395 ÷ _____ Minutes reading time = rate _____   97

Name _____

Directions: *Circle the correct answer.*

_____ %

_____ wpm

1. True or False: Scientists have finally come to understand all there is to know about the human ear.

2. True or False: Hearing takes place in the brain.

3. Extremely loud noises can damage our ears, especially if the noises are __?__ .
   - **a.** unexpected
   - **b.** unusual
   - **c.** unexplained
   - **d.** unidentifiable

4. Scientists say that a normal person can distinguish __?__ .
   - **a.** nearly one thousand sounds
   - **b.** nearly one-half million sounds
   - **c.** one million sounds
   - **d.** two million sounds

5. Hearing starts with __?__ .
   - **a.** an electrical impulse
   - **b.** hydraulic pressure
   - **c.** sound waves

6. True or False: The ear contains no bones.

7. This article compares the ear to __?__ .
   - **a.** a machine
   - **b.** a drum
   - **c.** a sound studio

Name _____

Directions: *Circle or write the correct answer.*

_____ %

_____ wpm

1. True or False: Winds quickly move entire sand dunes for great distances.

2. How does wind move sand grains?
    a. It flies the grains through the air.
    b. It bounces the grains along.
    c. It pushes one layer of sand at a time.
    d. It pushes against the base of the dune causing all the grains to shift.

3. True or False: There are three general types of sand dunes.

4. True or False: The Great Sand Dunes are in the Western United States.

5. What was God's reason for putting sandy dunes along the sea coasts?

_____

6. Why won't the world's most famous dune—Kill Devil Hill—ever move again?
    a. It washed out to sea.
    b. It blew away.
    c. It was rooted by grasses.
    d. It was covered by a building.

7. True or False: All sand dunes travel.

8. True or False: Once an entire village was buried by sand dunes.

Number of words: 430 ÷ _____ Minutes reading time = rate _____   101

Directions: *Circle or write the correct answer.*

1. Where does the rainbow appear in relation to the sun?

   a. beneath the sun   **c.** beside the sun

   b. opposite the sun   **d.** over the sun

2. True or False: Sunlight is made up of the colors of the rainbow.

3. How many colors are in the rainbow? _____

4. What serve as prisms to make a rainbow?

   a. sunbeams   **b.** rain clouds   **c.** raindrops

5. True or False: Snowflakes do not produce a rainbow because each snowflake is different.

6. Why does the rainbow that you see in the water from a sprinkler or a waterfall seem so dim?

   a. The water drops are so far from the sun.

   b. The water drops move so quickly.

   c. The water drops are so small.

   d. The water drops are so close together.

7. Yes or No: Would you be likely to see a rainbow on an overcast day?

8. Why are rainbows curved?

   a. The sun is curved.

   b. Clouds are curved.

   c. Raindrops are curved.

Bonus: Name all the colors of the rainbow.

_____

_____

Name _____

Directions: *Circle or write the correct answer.*

1. Mollusks need "shell houses" because they have no

    _____.

2. Mollusks got their name from a Latin word which means

    _____.

3. True or False: A mollusk has a "mantle" on its back and sides which secretes the special liquid that hardens into its shell.

4. True or False: Many types of mollusks can unhook themselves from their shells.

5. Mollusks with hinged shells are called __?__ .
    - **a.** conches
    - **b.** bivalves
    - **c.** gastropods
    - **d.** snails

6. Give one example named in this selection of a mollusk which has a hinged shell.

    _____

7. There are how many species of mollusks?
    - **a.** 700
    - **b.** 7,000
    - **c.** 70,000
    - **d.** 700,000

8. Name one reason why men have gathered shells throughout the years.

    _____

Name _____

Directions: *Circle or write the correct answer.*

_____ %

_____ wpm

1. True or False: The first person in the United States to volunteer to ascend in a balloon was a young boy.

2. The first hot-air balloon voyage with people aboard took place in __?__ .
   - **a.** Maryland
   - **b.** France
   - **c.** California
   - **d.** Mexico

3. Joseph and Jacques Étienne Montgolfier designed hot-air balloons. In this article, these brothers were compared to what other famous brothers?

   _____

4. What scientific principle makes it possible for these balloons to rise?
   - **a.** What goes up must come down.
   - **b.** Like poles repel.
   - **c.** Hot air rises.
   - **d.** Gases contract when they are cooled.

5. Which word does not have anything to do with a hot-air balloon?
   - **a.** gondola
   - **b.** rudder
   - **c.** gas burner
   - **d.** nylon

6. What will happen if the air inside one of these balloons cools?
   - **a.** The balloon will descend.
   - **b.** The balloon will rise higher.
   - **c.** The balloon will burst.
   - **d.** The balloon will go off course.

7. Select the most favorable spot to participate in the sport of ballooning.
   - **a.** Western plains
   - **b.** Rocky Mountains
   - **c.** Boston, Massachusetts
   - **d.** Niagara Falls

8. True or False: Where a balloon lands depends on the wind.

Bonus: Of what material are today's hot-air balloons made?

_____

Number of words: 450 ÷ _____ Minutes reading time = rate _____   107

_____ %

_____ wpm

Directions: *Circle or write the correct answer.*

1. What state suffers the most crop damage from hail?
   - **a.** North Carolina
   - **b.** Kansas
   - **c.** Colorado
   - **d.** Florida

2. True or False: Hailstones can be as big as baseballs.

3. True or False: Hailstones always melt as soon as they hit the ground.

4. True or False: Hailstorms only occur in North America.

5. Which of these states probably has the most hailstorms?
   - **a.** Florida
   - **b.** Wyoming
   - **c.** Texas
   - **d.** New York

6. The largest hailstone on record measured _?_.
   - **a.** 7 inches
   - **b.** 17 inches
   - **c.** 27 inches
   - **d.** 37 inches

7. True or False: Even tropical islands in the South Pacific have occasional hailstorms.

8. True or False: Hail forms when ice builds around a nucleus of dust or moisture.

Directions: *Circle the correct answer.*

1. True or False: A porcupine can shoot his quills at an attacker from a short distance away.

2. How many quills does a porcupine have on his back and sides?
   - **a.** 10,000
   - **b.** 3,000
   - **c.** 30,000
   - **d.** 13,000

3. Mountain lions can hunt porcupines successfully, but they must attack only __?__ .
   - **a.** the feet
   - **b.** the head and belly
   - **c.** the tail
   - **d.** the back

4. True or False: Porcupine quills can kill an attacker by going deep into the throat and head.

5. Porcupine quills are covered with __?__ .
   - **a.** tiny blades
   - **b.** poison
   - **c.** soft fur
   - **d.** skin

6. When we are faced with temptation, we, like the porcupine's attacker, must __?__ .
   - **a.** take a chance
   - **b.** act quickly
   - **c.** think about the danger

Name _____

Directions: *Circle or write the correct answer.*

1. True or False: This author appreciates beavers.

2. What would happen to a beaver's teeth if the
   beaver stopped gnawing on trees?
      a. The teeth would grow longer and longer.
      b. The teeth would get soft and fall out.
      c. The teeth would become dull and ineffective.
      d. The teeth would grow brittle and break off.

3. True or False: Beavers do more good for the environment than
   they do harm.

4. Besides its teeth, what other part of its body does a beaver use for
   building?

   _____

5. True or False: Beaver dams float on top of the water.

6. What are beaver dams made of?
      a. hard mud only
      b. mud, stones, and branches
      c. grass and twigs
      d. smooth, round stones

7. Which is *not* true about a beaver's home?
      a. It can be large enough for a man to crawl into.
      b. It is dry though it is underwater.
      c. It stores nuts and seeds, the beaver's food supply.
      d. It lies half in the water and half on the bank.

8. True or False: Beavers are relatives of the rat.

Number of words: 470 ÷ _____ Minutes reading time = rate _____ 113

Name _____

_____ %

_____ wpm

Directions: *Match the famous horse with the phrase which best identifies it.*

____ 1. Traveller

____ 2. Comanche

____ 3. Black Jack

____ 4. Winchester

  a. Carried General Sheridan to his troops

  b. Marched in the funeral of President Kennedy

  c. Sole survivor at the Battle of Little Big Horn

  d. Robert E. Lee's horse

Directions: *Circle or write the correct answer.*

5. What great leader founded a town in honor of his beloved horse, Bucephalus?

_____

6. Which general did Thomas Buchanan write a poem about?
    a. General Robert E. Lee
    b. General Philip Sheridan
    c. General George Custer
    d. General George Washington

7. True or False: The last great cavalry charge on record took place during World War II.

8. True or False: Once the Marines made a horse an honorary sergeant.

9. Which statement was *not* implied in this article?
    a. In times past, horses were vital members of the military.
    b. Today, horses are making a comeback in the military services.
    c. Today, military horses participate in some ceremonies.

Number of words: 490 ÷ ____ Minutes reading time = rate ____   115

Name _____

Directions: *Circle or write the correct answer.*

1. Mackinac Island is part of what state?

   _____ %

   _____ wpm

   _____

2. Why did residents of Mackinac Island not
   allow cars on the island?

   a. Cars are noisy and would disturb the peace.
   b. Mackinac Island has no roads.
   c. Cars would frighten the fur-bearing animals.
   d. Cars take up more room than bicycles.

3. The only forms of transportation on Mackinac Island are
   bicycles and

   _____.

4. Would Mackinac Island be considered large or small?

   _____

5. What product made Mackinac Island well known and brought
   many people to the island?

   _____

6. True or False: Indians once inhabited Mackinac Island.

7. Who made Mackinac Island his headquarters?

   a. Jacob Astor, a Jesuit missionary
   b. John Astor, a British soldier
   c. John Jacob Astor, an American millionaire
   d. John Jacob Astor, a French fur trader

8. True or False: After trade declined, Mackinac Island became a
   vacation resort and tourist attraction.

Name _____

Directions: *Circle or write the correct answer.*

1. Which of the following descriptions of a
   windmill was *not* used in this article?
      a. a Texas lady in her bonnet
      b. tall as a massed schooner
      c. nearly perfect ecological machine
      d. skyscraper of the plains

2. What energy source is used to run a windmill?

   _____

3. True or False: The author can remember seeing windmills when
   he was a boy.

4. During World War II the United States built the world's biggest
   windmill in what state?
      a. Kansas   **c.** Texas
      b. Vermont   **d.** Oregon

5. True or False: Windmills have never become popular anywhere
   except in the United States.

6. America would probably still have millions of windmills if it
   weren't for __?__.
      a. ecology   **c.** economy
      b. electricity   **d.** education

7. Yes or No: Do energy experts agree with the author's opinion that
   windmills could help save fuel resources?

Name _____

Directions: *Circle or write the correct answer.*

_____ %

_____ wpm

1. True or False: The theories of science can change.

2. Why was Israel the only early civilization that believed the earth is a sphere?
   - **a.** Israel had the Bible.
   - **b.** Israel was a very advanced civilization.
   - **c.** The telescope was invented in Israel.
   - **d.** The first person to sail around the world was an Israelite.

3. When Moses wrote in Genesis about the "firmament of the heaven," he was saying that __?__.
   - **a.** the earth is a sphere
   - **b.** the universe is expanding
   - **c.** the stars are innumerable
   - **d.** Heaven is above the earth

4. Who first used a telescope to study the stars?
   - **a.** Aristotle
   - **c.** Plato
   - **b.** Galileo
   - **d.** Einstein

5. True or False: Today we know that there are not only billions of stars, but there are also billions of galaxies.

6. What is the oldest book in the Bible?
   - **a.** Genesis
   - **c.** Job
   - **b.** Proverbs
   - **d.** Jonah

7. True or False: Science has proven the Bible to be scientifically inaccurate.

Name _____

Directions: *Circle or write the correct answer.*

_____ %

_____ wpm

1. What part of the tulip is shipped to sellers all over the world?

_____

2. Who sells more tulips, The Netherlands or Japan?

_____

3. Why do farmers cut off tulip blossoms?
   a. to prevent disease
   b. to produce bigger bulbs
   c. to produce more bulbs
   d. to produce more blossoms

4. Where might flower-lovers see tulip blooms earlier?
   a. in America   **b.** in The Netherlands

5. After being harvested, tulip bulbs must be soaked in what?
   a. hot water   **c.** warm water
   b. cold water   **d.** fertilizer

6. If harvested tulip bulbs are small, what does the flower farmer do?
   a. replants them   **c.** sells them more cheaply
   b. throws them away   **d.** soaks them in cold water

7. Yes or No: Would Dutchmen have to chill tulip bulbs which were being sent to Alaska?

8. True or False: Single tulip bulbs once sold for thousands of dollars.

Number of words: 560 ÷ _____ Minutes reading time = rate _____   123

Name _____

Directions: *Circle or write the correct answer.*

1. True or False: Just recently researchers have been able to figure out what gives homing pigeons their sense of direction.

_____ %

_____ wpm

2. What people were using homing pigeons as messengers as early as 3000 B.C.?

    a. Egyptians   **b.** Greeks   **c.** Persians   **d.** Israelites

3. Which statement is *false?*

    a. Homing pigeons have been credited with winning battles.

    b. Homing pigeons were used in Greece to carry the names of Olympic winners.

    c. Bird racing is illegal.

    d. Some pigeons can fly for more than a thousand miles.

4. Which statement is *true?*

    a. "Homing" is an instinct.

    b. Homing pigeons lose their sense of direction when blindfolded.

    c. Homing pigeons fly fast, but for short distances.

    d. Homing pigeons never get lost.

5. What made pigeons more useful for delivering secret messages?

    a. magnetism   **c.** bird banding

    b. microphotography   **d.** bird racing

6. What was the only bird named in this article?

    a. G. I. Joe   **c.** Sutan of Baghdad

    b. Queen Elizabeth   **d.** Paul Reuter

7. What might possibly throw a homing pigeon off course?

    a. strange landscapes   **c.** strong winds

    b. loud noises   **d.** thick clouds

8. True or False: From this article, you can assume that a pigeon's *loft* is its home.

Number of words: 570 ÷ _____ Minutes reading time = rate _____   125

Directions: *Circle or write the correct answer.*

1. How do scientists rate really good ice cream?

   _____ %

   _____ wpm

   a. mellow   **c.** smooth
   b. delicious   **d.** cool

2. What does *not* contribute to making the best ice cream?
   a. smooth texture
   b. right-sized ice crystals
   c. carbonated water

3. At the 1964 World's Fair, Dr. Arbuckle introduced a new kind of ice cream. What was it?
   a. rhubarb ice cream   **c.** grape ice pops
   b. sweet potato ice cream   **d.** frozen yogurt

4. The first ice-cream cone was ___?___.
   a. a Syrian waffle   **c.** invented by Robert Green
   b. made from surplus cream **d.** invented by Dr. Arbuckle

5. True or False: The story of ice cream is one of long, scientific investigation.

6. What did Little Miss Muffett eat that you might also eat in an ice pop?
   a. cheese   **b.** curds   **c.** whey   **d.** cream

7. Why can the story of ice cream be called "serendipitous"?
   a. Many delicious ice-cream inventions were made at World's Fairs.
   b. Many delicious ice-cream inventions were happy accidents.
   c. Many delicious ice-cream inventions made their inventors wealthy.
   d. Many delicious ice-cream inventions are still popular today.

8. Which World's Fair is *not* mentioned in this article?
   a. New York World's Fair
   b. St. Louis World's Fair
   c. Seattle World's Fair

Name _____

Directions: *Circle or write the correct answer.*

_____ %

_____ wpm

1. True or False: Some squids are known to be as small as a dime.

2. True or False: Some squids will even attack huge whales.

3. How many arms does a squid have, counting large and small arms?

    a. 10   **b.** 8   **c.** 6   **d.** 2

4. True or False: Squids are fussy eaters and will not eat most things in the sea.

5. The article compares a squid to a __?__ .

    a. helicopter   **b.** submarine   **c.** shark   **d.** jellyfish

6. Does a squid usually swim backward or forward? _____

7. How does a squid fool his enemy?

    a. by darting quickly downward

    b. by playing dead

    c. by squirting ink into a squidlike shape

    d. by floating backward

8. If not many Americans eat squid, why do American fisherman haul in tons of it each year?

    a. to sell as fish bait   **c.** to protect other fish

    b. to sell to scientists   **d.** to export to other countries

9. What do scientists think might be the secret of the squid's speed and adaptability?

    a. the ink it shoots off   **c.** its large nervous system

    b. its photophores   **d.** its long arms

10. Which of the following is the *least* like a squid?

    a. octopus   **b.** cuttlefish   **c.** dolphin

Bonus: What do we call the group of boneless, soft-bodied animals to which the squid belongs?

_____

Number of words: 640 ÷ ____ Minutes reading time = rate ____   129

Name _____

Directions: *Circle or write the correct answer.*

1. True or False: This expedition was like a
   graduation exercise after six summers at camp.

   _____ %

   _____ wpm

2. In what state did this expedition take place?

   a. Maine   **b.** Oregon   **c.** Wyoming   **d.** New York

3. Taking canoes out of the water in one place and carrying them
   overland to the next place is called __?__.

   a. a caravan **b.** a portage   **c.** an expedition **d.** a lift

4. What is another name for swift, racing water?

   a. falls   **b.** rapids   **c.** cataracts   **d.** white caps

5. Which answer does not have anything to do with this story?
   a. Camp Kennebec
   b. Allagash Wilderness Waterway
   c. Lake Erie
   d. Fort Kent

6. Which of the following did the canoeists *not* use to propel their
   canoes during this expedition?

   a. poles   **b.** paddles   **c.** sails   **d.** motors

7. Why couldn't the campers eat food which had been touched by
   river water?

   _____

8. What made the trip easier for these canoeists?
   a. Their camping gear was flown to each campsite.
   b. They were all old and experienced.
   c. They encountered no rough waters.
   d. Their canoe never turned over.

9. This unforgettable journey lasted how many days? _____

10. True or False: One day the canoeists covered 28 miles.

Number of words: 650 ÷ _____ Minutes reading time = rate _____   131

Name _____

Directions: *Circle or write the correct answer.*

_____ %

_____ wpm

1. Which of the following characteristics of
   reindeer is *not* mentioned in this article?

   a. long legs   **c.** sharp eyes

   b. broad hooves   **d.** double-layered coat

2. The nomads of northern Scandinavia and Siberia are called __?__ .

   a. Eskimos   **c.** Norsemen

   b. Lapps   **d.** Rangifers

3. When a reindeer is killed, no part of it is wasted. What are its
   antlers and bones used for?

   a. soup   **b.** pet food   **c.** tools   **d.** jewelry

4. True or False: A reindeer's favorite food is berries.

5. True or False: A harnessed reindeer can outrun a horse in a race.

6. *Caribou* is the French word for the reindeer that are native to
   what country?

   _____

7. If Rudolph the Red-Nosed Reindeer is pictured at Christmas with
   antlers, Rudolph is __?__ .

   a. a male reindeer

   b. a female reindeer

8. In which of the following places would you *not* be able to find
   reindeer?

   a. Alaska   **c.** Canada

   b. Soviet Union   **d.** France

Name _____

Directions: *Circle or write the correct answer.*

_____ %

_____ wpm

1. The boy in this article lives in a ghost town
   in __?__.
   a. Alaska   c. North Dakota
   b. Colorado   d. Canada

2. What is a good reason why this young man drives huskies from
   only mid-December to mid-April?

   _____

3. How many dogs are harnessed to pull a sled? _____

4. A dog team is controlled by __?__.
   a. a whip   c. the driver's voice
   b. the reins   d. the lead dog

5. What is another name for the driver of a dogsled?

   _____

6. True or False: A dog team can pull a load weighing one ton on a
   good trail.

7. Where is the driver positioned while driving the sled?
   a. on a seat behind the sled   c. in the sled
   b. on the sled's runners

8. True or False: Dogs can tell if the driver is inexperienced.

9. What characteristic best qualifies a dog for lead dog?
   a. responsibility   c. authority
   b. strength   d. experience

Bonus: The dogs owned by the family in this story are a cross between
what two kinds of dogs?

_____

Number of words: 665 ÷ _____ Minutes reading time = rate _____   135

Directions: *Circle or write the correct answer.*

_____ %

_____ wpm

1. Which of the following animals is *not* listed as a Trail-Maker?
   - **a.** deer
   - **b.** moose
   - **c.** antelope
   - **d.** elk

2. What is the smallest Trail-Maker? _____

3. True or False: Deer have very poor hearing, smell, and sight.

4. What nickname has been given to the deer?

   _____

5. Bucks grow a new prong on their antlers __?__ .
   - **a.** each month
   - **b.** each year
   - **c.** every 2 years
   - **d.** every 5 years

6. Who were the first people to follow the paths of the Trail-Makers?
   - **a.** trappers and hunters
   - **b.** gold seekers
   - **c.** railroad builders
   - **d.** mountain climbers

7. True or False: The Trail-Makers always find the shortest, easiest route.

Directions: *Circle or write the correct answer.*

_____ %

_____ wpm

1. Circle the adjectives below that describe the elk.
   - **a.** clumsy
   - **b.** swift
   - **c.** powerful
   - **d.** big

2. Why is the elk called Trees-in-the-Head?
   - **a.** He stands as tall as some trees.
   - **b.** His huge antlers look like trees on top of his head.
   - **c.** His antlers scrape the trees as he runs by them.
   - **d.** He often gets branches caught in his antlers.

3. During what season do the bull elk fight? _____

4. What animal is referred to in the story as the monarch of the wilderness?

   _____

5. Which of the following is the *best* description of the moose?
   - **a.** tall and black, with long, thin antlers
   - **b.** almost black, with long legs and broad, wide antlers
   - **c.** brown, with wide hooves and tall antlers
   - **d.** black, with short legs and long, thin antlers

6. True or False: The tassel of fur that hangs from a moose's throat is called the "beard."

7. Where does the caribou make trails?

   _____

8. Circle the animals that were *not* mentioned in this story.
   - **a.** antelope
   - **b.** bull
   - **c.** reindeer
   - **d.** buffalo

Number of words: 665 ÷ _____ Minutes reading time = rate _____   139

Directions: *Circle or write the correct answer.*

1. True or False: Monkeys enjoy swimming.

2. Which of the following statements accurately describes the monkey chain?

    a. The smallest monkey held on to the tree with his hands, then another monkey held his tail, and so on.

    b. The monkeys formed a chain on the ground by holding hands, then the first monkey climbed the tree and hung from a branch.

    c. The first monkey hung by his tail from the tree, then the next monkey climbed over him, wrapping his tail around him, and so on.

3. True or False: The last monkey on the chain pushed his hands against the ground to start the chain swinging toward a tree on the opposite bank.

4. On what continent did this story take place?

_____

5. The monkeys in this story were a good example of __?__ .

    a. independence   **c.** teamwork

    b. courage   **d.** leadership

6. Circle the adjectives that describe the monkeys in this story.

    a. noisy   **c.** cooperative

    b. confused   **d.** intelligent

7. The monkeys in this story were compared to __?__ .

    a. an army   **b.** a circus   **c.** a sports team

Name _____

Directions: *Circle or write the correct answer.*

1. Which two of the following weather conditions can cause a flash flood?
   - **a.** melting snow
   - **b.** strong winds
   - **c.** high seas
   - **d.** heavy rain

2. True or False: You are safe inside a car during a flash flood.

3. If you are in the city during a flash flood you should not go near __?__ .
   - **a.** skyscrapers
   - **b.** flagpoles
   - **c.** street drains

4. Where there is thunder, there is _____.

5. Circle the statement that is *false*.
   - **a.** Lightning can travel through phone wires.
   - **b.** Water attracts electricity.
   - **c.** Lightning does not strike trees.
   - **d.** Metal conducts electricity.

6. True or False: You should not lie flat on the ground during a lightning storm.

7. During a flash flood, you should be at the _____ of a hill.
   During a lightning storm, you should be at the _____ of a hill.

Bonus: What state receives the greatest number of lightning strikes?

_____

Directions: *Circle or write the correct answer.*

_____ %

_____ wpm

1. What part of the owl's body collects sounds?
   a. the feathers around his eyes
   b. the feathers that cover his ears
   c. the wide pupils in his eyes

2. What is the owl's favorite meal? _____

3. True or False: The great horned owl cannot see at night.

4. What makes the owl's wings silent?
   a. saucer shaped feathers
   b. extremely large feathers
   c. soft, downy edges on the feathers
   d. very few feathers

5. True or False: The owl's stomach separates any bones, fur, and teeth that he swallows from the meat.

6. When does the great horned owl sleep? _____

7. When does the great horned owl hunt? _____

8. Circle the facts that were *not* given in this selection.
   a. The great horned owl needs big ears.
   b. The great horned owl has yellow eyes.
   c. The great horned owl can eat small rodents whole.
   d. The great horned owl can be found throughout North America.

Name _____

Directions: *Circle or write the correct answer.*

1. Where is the Treetops Hotel located?

    _____ %

    _____ wpm

    a. New Delhi, India
    b. Kenya, Africa
    c. Brisbane, Australia
    d. Nigeria, Africa

2. What lures all the beasts to the hotel?

    a. the provided shelter **c.** the food offered by guests

    b. the water hole **d.** the shade provided by the building

3. Which animal is first in the animal "pecking order"?

    _____

4. What lady found out that she had become a queen while visiting the Treetops?

    _____

5. Elephants may be large, but they have a soft heart for __?__ .

    a. sick and wounded rhinos
    b. sick and wounded comrades
    c. sick and wounded natives
    d. sick and wounded birds

6. What large animal is as light on its feet as a polo pony?

    a. elephant **b.** rhinoceros **c.** buffalo **d.** hippopotamus

7. What animal has such a tough mouth that it can eat dried branches and huge thorns?

    a. elephant **b.** rhinoceros **c.** buffalo **d.** hippopotamus

8. True or False: The buffalo is considered by many to be the most dangerous animal to hunt because of his speed and power.

9. Yes or No: Treetops would be a welcome place for hunters to stay.

Number of words: 900 ÷ _____ Minutes reading time = rate _____   147

Name _____

Directions: *Circle the correct answer.*

1. What does *echinoderm* mean?
   - **a.** five arms
   - **b.** spiny skin
   - **c.** star-shaped
   - **d.** smooth skin

2. True or False: All starfish are yellow and have five arms.

3. Under a microscope, the spines on a starfish would look like __?__ .
   - **a.** tiny jaws
   - **b.** thin tubes
   - **c.** sharp points
   - **d.** short hairs

4. True or False: The starfish's mouth is on the bottom side of his body.

5. What part of his body does the starfish put inside the oyster shell?
   - **a.** his arm
   - **b.** his mouth
   - **c.** his stomach

6. True or False: The starfish sucks the oyster out of his shell before eating him.

7. True or False: Red, pink, orange, and yellow are the most common starfish colors.

8. How long does a starfish usually live?
   - **a.** 10 years
   - **b.** 15 years
   - **c.** 5 years
   - **d.** 1 year

Name _____

Directions: *Circle or write the correct answer.*

_____ %

_____ wpm

1. What part of his body does T.D. use to dig?
   a. his legs   **b.** his mouth   **c.** his head

2. Why does T.D. line the inside of his house with silk?
   a. for comfort and beauty
   b. to catch insects
   c. to keep his home warm and dry
   d. to keep the walls from caving in

3. T.D. gets the silk he uses __?__ .
   a. from inside his body
   b. from the plants near his home
   c. from the caterpillars he eats
   d. from other spiders

4. What is the trapdoor made of?
   a. mud covered with silk
   b. grass covered with silk
   c. silk covered with moss
   d. silk only

5. What does T.D. use to camouflage the trapdoor?

   _____

6. True or False: The trapdoor automatically slides open when an insect crosses it.

7. True or False: Sometimes T.D. has to hold his door shut to keep out an attacker.

8. Which of the following is a myriapod?
   a. spider   **b.** centipede   **c.** wasp   **d.** beetle

Number of words: 985 ÷ _____ Minutes reading time = rate _____   151

Directions: *Circle or write the correct answer.*

1. What President sent Lewis and Clark on
   their expedition?

   _____ %

   _____ wpm

   _____

2. What did Lewis and Clark do during the
   winter months?
   - **a.** lived in an Indian settlement
   - **c.** continued their explorations
   - **b.** stayed in a fort that they built
   - **d.** lived in a cave

3. Choose the answer which does *not* describe Sacagawea.
   - **a.** a Shoshoni Indian
   - **c.** a poor guide
   - **b.** the wife of a French trapper
   - **d.** an Indian captive

4. Lewis and Clark needed horses to cross over land. Fortunately, __?__.
   - **a.** they had brought some with them
   - **b.** there were plenty of wild horses to catch
   - **c.** Indians were willing to trade horses for trinkets
   - **d.** fur traders swapped horses for furs

5. To Indians, a woman with a party of men is __?__.
   - **a.** a sign of peace
   - **b.** an insult
   - **c.** a sign of weakness
   - **d.** a warning signal

6. True or False: Lewis and Clark explored the Missouri in a canoe.

7. Which of the following rivers was *not* mentioned in this article?
   - **a.** Missouri River
   - **c.** Snake River
   - **b.** Columbia River
   - **d.** Arkansas River

8. In what state were Lewis and Clark when they finally reached the
   Pacific?
   - **a.** Oregon
   - **b.** California
   - **c.** Washington
   - **d.** Missouri

9. The Lewis and Clark expedition took __?__.
   - **a.** more than five years
   - **b.** less than five years

Number of words: 1,015 ÷ _____ Minutes reading time = rate _____ 153

Name _____

Directions: *Circle or write the correct answer.*

1. As a boy, Wilfred Grenfell lived in what country?

   _____

   _____ %

   _____ wpm

2. Wilfred Grenfell accepted Christ as his personal Savior __?__.
   - **a.** when he was a very young boy
   - **b.** when he was in college studying medicine
   - **c.** when he was on a hospital boat in the North Sea
   - **d.** when he was floating on an ice pan

3. Wilfred Grenfell served as a missionary doctor to Labrador. Labrador is in what country?
   - **a.** England   **b.** France   **c.** Canada   **d.** America

4. Which of the following facts is *not* true of Wilfred Grenfell?
   - **a.** He discovered a cure for frostbite.
   - **b.** He founded schools and orphanages.
   - **c.** He built hospitals.
   - **d.** He wrote books.
   - **e.** He became a knight.

5. In what body of water was Dr. Grenfell afloat?
   - **a.** Yukon River   **b.** North Sea   **c.** Hudson Bay   **d.** Pacific Ocean

6. Chewing on the rubber band __?__.
   - **a.** took Dr. Grenfell's mind off his dangerous plight
   - **b.** comforted Dr. Grenfell's hungry stomach
   - **c.** saved Dr. Grenfell's life
   - **d.** quenched Dr. Grenfell's thirst

7. Circle all the words that describe Dr. Grenfell as this article presents him.
   - **a.** industrious   **c.** prayerful   **e.** dedicated
   - **b.** wealthy   **d.** dismayed   **f.** helpful

Bonus: For how many years did Wilfred Grenfell serve God as a missionary?

_____

Quiz Answer Key

Quiz 1 *Pilgrims, Indians, and Thanksgiving*—p. 1
1. c
2. true
3. c
4. false
5. b
6. b

Quiz 2 *Hippos at Home*—p. 3
1. horse
2. b
3. a
4. true
Bonus: false
5. b
6. b
7. b

Quiz 3 *The Incredible Ear*—p. 5
1. false
2. true
3. a
4. b
5. c
6. false
7. a

Quiz 4 *Nature's Sandpiles*—p. 7
1. false
2. b
3. false
4. true
5. protect the land from the sea
6. c
7. false
8. true

Quiz 5 *Raindrop Miracles*—p. 9
1. b
2. true
3. six
4. c
5. false
6. c
7. no
8. c
Bonus: red, orange, yellow, green, blue, violet

Quiz 6 *Mollusk Mansions*—p. 11
1. skeletons/ bones
2. soft
3. true
4. false
5. b
6. clam or oyster
7. c
8. to use as money, to make jewelry, to admire

Quiz 7 *Up and Away in a Hot-Air Balloon*—p. 13
1. true
2. b
3. Wright Brothers
4. c
Bonus: nylon
5. b
6. a
7. a
8. true

Quiz 8 *Summer Ice Storms*—p. 15
1. b
2. true
3. false
4. false
5. b
6. b
7. true
8. true

Quiz 9 *The Pincushion*—p. 17
1. false
2. c
3. b
4. true
5. a
6. c

Quiz 10 *Beaver Business*—p. 19
1. true
2. a
3. true
4. tail
5. false
6. b
7. c
8. true

Quiz 11 *The Valiant Horse*—p. 21
1. d
2. c
3. b
4. a
5. Alexander the Great
6. b
7. true
8. true
9. b

Quiz 12 *Michigan's Magic Island*—p. 24
1. Michigan
2. a
3. horses
4. small
5. furs
6. true
7. c
8. true

Quiz 13 *The Windmill: Energy's Friend*—p. 26
1. d
2. wind
3. true
4. b
5. false
6. b
7. yes

Quiz 14 *The Unchanging Bible and Science*—p. 29
1. true
2. a
3. b
4. b
5. true
6. c
7. false

Quiz 15 *The Blossoming Tulip Business*—p. 31
1. bulb
2. The Netherlands
3. b
4. a
5. a
6. a
7. no
8. true

Quiz 16 *Homing Pigeon Heroes*—p. 34
1. false
2. a
3. c
4. a
5. b
6. a
7. c
8. true

Quiz 17 *The Real Scoop about Ice Cream*—*p. 37*
1. a
2. c
3. b
4. a
5. false
6. c
7. b
8. c

Quiz 18 *Squid Tricks*—*p. 40*
1. true
2. true
3. a
4. false
5. b
6. backward
7. c
8. a
9. c
10. c

Bonus: mollusks or cephalopods

Quiz 19 *Riding the Rapids*—*p. 43*
1. true
2. a
3. b
4. b
5. c
6. d
7. polluted
8. a
9. 18
10. true

Quiz 20 *Red-Nosed Reindeer*—*p. 46*
1. c
2. b
3. c
4. false
5. true
6. Canada
7. b
8. d

Quiz 21 *Huskies in the Rockies*—*p. 49*
1. b
2. there is snow
3. 13
4. c
5. musher
6. false
7. b
8. true
9. a

Bonus: Alaskan malamutes and Siberian huskies

Quiz 22 *Trail-Makers, Part 1*—*p. 52*
1. c
2. deer
3. false
4. White-Tail
5. b
6. a
7. true

Quiz 23 *Trail-Makers, Part 2*—*p. 55*
1. a, c, d
2. b
3. fall
4. moose
5. b
6. false
7. in the North
8. b, c

Quiz 24 *A Bridge of Monkeys*—*p. 58*
1. false
2. c
3. true
4. South America
5. c
6. a, c, d
7. a

Quiz 25 *Storm Warnings*—*p. 61*
1. a, d
2. false
3. c
4. lightning
5. c
6. true
7. top, bottom

Bonus: Florida

Quiz 26 *Who Goes There?*—*p. 65*
1. a
2. skunk
3. false
4. c
5. true
6. during the day
7. at night
8. b, d

Quiz 27 *Spy on Wild Animals from a Treetop Hotel*—*p. 69*
1. b
2. b
3. elephant
4. Queen Elizabeth
5. b
6. b
7. b
8. false
9. no

Quiz 28 *The Oyster Thief*—*p. 73*
1. b
2. false
3. a
4. true
5. c
6. false
7. true
8. c

Quiz 29 *The Trap-Door Spider*—*p. 77*
1. b
2. c
3. a
4. a
5. moss
6. false
7. true
8. b

Quiz 30 *Lewis and Clark Open the Door to the West*—*p. 81*
1. Thomas Jefferson
2. b
3. c
4. c
5. a
6. false
7. d
8. a
9. b

Quiz 31 *Grenfell of Labrador*—*p. 86*
1. England
2. b
3. c
4. a
5. c
6. b
7. a, c, e, f

Bonus: 40 years